Benjamin Titus Roberts

First Lessons on Money

Benjamin Titus Roberts

First Lessons on Money

ISBN/EAN: 9783744730624

Printed in Europe, USA, Canada, Australia, Japan

Cover: Foto ©Suzi / pixelio.de

More available books at **www.hansebooks.com**

FIRST LESSONS

ON

MONEY

BY

B. T. ROBERTS, A. M.

———

A man should make it a part of his religion
to see that his country is well governed.
—*William Penn.*

———

ROCHESTER, N. Y.,
1886.

Entered according to Act of Congress in the year 1886, by
B. T. ROBERTS,
In the Office of the Librarian of Congress at Washington.

PREFACE.

I HAVE written this little book because I felt I must. It was begun several years ago when silver was demonetized. It was not finished because the hope was cherished that it would not be needed. But as it has become evident that the money question will not be settled until THE PEOPLE settle it, this unpretending volume has been published in the hope that it may help them to settle it properly and speedily.

For the last twenty-five years I have mingled freely with the common people, from New England to California, and from Dakota to Texas.

I have witnessed the distress that the bad management of our finances by our National Government has produced, and the injury that has been done by the same cause to our religious and benevolent enterprises.

Some of the views presented are in advance

of the times; but we trust they will be seen to be sound.

We ask a careful and candid perusal.

B. T. ROBERTS,
Rochester, N. Y., May, 1886.

CONTENTS.

CHAPTER I.
THE SUBJECT COMPREHENSIBLE.   PAGE 8

Money a Human Invention, - - - - - 8
Wrong Instruction, - - - - - - 10

CHAPTER II.
IMPORTANCE OF THE SUBJECT.   12

All Interests Affected, - - - - - - 13
Losses From Bad Management, - - - - 15

CHAPTER III.
MONEY NECESSARY.   17

Difficulties of Barter, - - - - - - 18
Mill and Gibbon quoted, - - - - - 20

CHAPTER IV.
WHAT IS MONEY?   23

Prof. Walker, Dr. Ely quoted, - - - - 24
Functions of Money, - - - - - - 25

CHAPTER V.
MATERIAL OF MONEY.   28

Leather Money, - - - - - - - 29
"Watered Stock," - - - - - - - 30
General Choice, - - - - - - - 32

CHAPTER VI.
GOLD AND SILVER. 34

National Debts,	34
Stock of Gold and Silver,	35
Value of Debts Doubled,	36

CHAPTER VII.
SILVER. 40

Early use of Silver,	41
Fluctuations of Value,	42
Adam Smith quoted,	44
Double Standard,	45
Ratio of Value,	49
Needless Fear,	50
More Gold than Silver,	52
Official Statements,	53

CHAPTER VIII.
PAPER MONEY. 58

Its Advantages,	59
Macaulay quoted,	59
Preferences of the People,	65

CHAPTER IX.
COINING MONEY. 67

Our Constitution,	68
Jefferson quoted,	69
Should be Issued by Congress,	70
Prof. Jevons quoted,	71
National Bank Bills,	72
Interest paid National Banks,	73

CONTENTS. vii.

Capital Released, - - - - - - - 75
Currency Inflated, - - - - - - 76
"Fiat Money," - - - - - - - 76

CHAPTER X.
BASIS OF PAPER MONEY. 82

Venetian System, - - - - - 83
The Bank of England, - - 85
The Proper Basis, - - - - - 88

CHAPTER XI.
BANKS. 90

Their Functions, - - - - - 91
Are Profitable. - - - - - - - 93
The Chemical Bank - - - - - 96

CHAPTER XII.
AMOUNT OF MONEY NEEDED. 99

Fraud Encouraged, - - - - - 100
"Innocent Holders" - - - - - 102
Letter to the President, - - - - 105
Contracting the Currency, - - - 107
Money Stock of Different Nations, - - 109

CHAPTER XIII.
"ELASTIC CURRENCY." 112

Going into Debt, - - - - - 113
Prof. Walker quoted, - - - - - 115

CHAPTER XIV.
DISTRIBUTION OF MONEY. 120

Division of Property, - - - - - 121

General Distribution, - - - - - - 123
Laws Favoring Great Fortunes, - - - - 127
Monopolies, - - - - - - - - 133

CHAPTER XV.
HOW TO MAKE MONEY. 143

Suggestions, - - - - - - - - 144
Rothschild's Maxims, - - - - - - 156

CHAPTER XVI.
CONCLUSION. 158

FIRST LESSONS ON MONEY.

CHAPTER I.

THE SUBJECT COMPREHENSIBLE.

MONEY is a human invention. Therefore the money question is a question that can be understood. What is made by man can be comprehended by man. The mechanism of a watch is intricate, but one who studies it with diligence may learn all about its construction and movements. So, whoever gives a proper attention to the machinery by which the wheels of trade and commerce are kept moving, can gain all the knowledge respecting it which is necessary for practical purposes.

With money itself every person in this country is familiar. He has used it from childhood. It is a great help towards understanding the theory of any thing to have some knowledge of the thing itself. A sail-

or, brought up on the ocean, can, with the same amount of study, get a much more accurate knowledge of navigation than he could if he had never seen a ship. So, one familiar with money, can understand the laws by which its issue and circulation should be governed, much more easily than he could if it was a new invention and for the first time coming into use.

The great embarrassment to a right understanding of the money question arises from the fact that what instruction the people generally have had upon it has been too often wrong. They have to unlearn in order to learn. Prejudice is worse to encounter than ignorance.

Mr. Walter Bagehot, one of the most distinguished writers on the money question, in the introduction to his able work entitled "Lombard Street," says: "A notion prevails that the money market is so impalpable that it can only be spoken of in very abstract words, and that, therefore, books on it must be exceedingly difficult. But I maintain that the money market is as concrete and real as any thing else; that it can be described in as plain words; that it is the writer's fault if what he says is not clear."

Then do not neglect to read upon this subject, under the impression that you never can know anything about it. You may understand it sufficiently well for all practical purposes, if you will. Think for yourself. Weigh with an unbiased judgment the statements and arguments which you read and hear.

The subject of money doubtless, is one that men of common mind and common education can comprehend. The terms used are familiar. They are not Greek and Latin, like those employed largely in treating of medicine. The subject is as easy to comprehend as almost any other subject of equal importance.

CHAPTER II.

IMPORTANCE OF THE SUBJECT.

IN enlightened countries, money is the creature of the government. Then the law-making power should understand the principles by which it should be created and regulated. In this country the power to make and execute the laws rests ultimately with the people. If the civil officers of one term act contrary to the wishes of the people, then, at the first opportunity, they select those who, they believe, can be relied upon to carry out their wishes. It is important then that THE PEOPLE should have correct views upon this subject.

In our present civilization the money interest affects every other interest, industrial, educational and religious. It is only a few years since this country, with every element of prosperity—peace at home and abroad, abundant harvests, and general health, suffered from a great prostration of business, occasioned by an unwise administration of our national finances. Manufactories, schools and churches were closed; and thousands of men, educated and uneducated, were tramping through a land abounding in supplies of food, seeking in vain for a place where they could earn their daily bread.

It is said that this paralysis of business was the necessary result of a great war. But France carried on in immediate succession a foreign war and a civil war, and not only had her own expenses to pay, but a large indemnity to pay to Germany; yet she suffered no such prostration. The success of her financial system was as marked as the failure of her armies.

The money question is now one of the great questions of the Nation. The natural resources of this country are but partially developed. Yet thousands who desire to work, are out of employment, because of the stagnation of business produced by the unwise administration of our national finances.

Every home, every church in the country, every business, every benevolent and religious enterprise, every missionary sent from us to heathen lands, feels the effect of the monetary measures of our Government.

If these measures are wise, then is there general prosperity,—if unwise, there is depression and discontent, distress and degeneration, and the wheels of progress are checked, or move backward.

Says Walter Bagehot, "A good system of currency will benefit the country and a bad system will hurt it." (Lombard Street, p. 22.)

Under our financial system, as administered, a great wrong is being done to the many for the benefit of the few. The rich are made immensely rich—those in moderate circumstances are reduced to poverty, and the poor are made poorer.

Yet there is not a natural element of prosperity that the country does not possess in great abundance. The distress results from artificial causes. The remedy is with the people.

Politicians cannot be trusted to take the right side of a question, until the people, in large and increasing numbers, are found upon that side.

Bad management of the finances of this country have cost the people an amount, which, if it could be definitely ascertained and stated in figures, would seem incredible. The losses from the failure of banks, and from the depreciation of property consequent upon mismanagement of our national finances, have been enormous.

There is no reason in the nature of things why the moneyed institutions of a country should not be as permanent as the government itself. Fluctuations there must be, consequent upon the variation in crops and in the state of affairs in the different nations with which we have commercial transactions; but these fluctuations need have but a narrow range. From year to year there should be no greater difference in the purchasing power of a dollar than that which arises from natural causes. There should be no prostration of business, no general distress growing out of money matters.

If a system of national finances is adopted that shall secure permanent prosperity, as far as money arrangements can do it, this result will be effected in answer to the persistent demands of the people.

The money power is a potent factor in our politics. It controls legislation until it becomes so oppressive that the people rise up against its control. It places men, simply because they are rich, in official positions for which they are totally unfitted.

But the intelligent convictions of a free people are stronger than the money power.

"The sober, second thought of a people," said Daniel Webster, "is seldom wrong and always efficient." A few years ago the constitution of California was amended in opposition to the active and energetic influence of the banks, the railroads, and a subsidized press. It was a spontaneous uprising of the people against the oppression of powerful moneyed corporations.

What is now needed is, that the people at large of the United States emancipate themselves from the prejudices that have been excited and fostered among them by the money power, and give to this question their independent, candid, sober, second thought.

CHAPTER III.

MONEY NECESSARY.

THE necessity for money arises out of the division of labor. The hermit who makes his own clothes, and shelter, raises his own provisions, travels on foot, and provides his own entertainment, needs no money. Even in a state of society in which the arts flourish to some extent, a good deal of trade can be carried on by barter. In the early settlement of this country those who began in the woods made maple sugar and potash, and took them to the older settlements, and exchanged them for food and clothes. This is the natural way of doing business. One man exchanges the product of his labor which he has in excess above his wants for the products of another man's labors which he has in excess above his wants. Thus something of real value is exchanged for something of real value. No risks are run, no loss is incurred.

But the disadvantages of this system of traffic are numerous.

It may be difficult for a man who has something to sell to find one who wishes to buy his goods and who has something to dispose of which he wants. "One man, we shall suppose, has more of a certain commodity than he himself has occasion for, while another has less. The former consequently would be glad to dispose of, and the latter to purchase, a part of this superfluity. But if this latter should chance to have nothing that the former stands in need of, no exchange can be made between them." (Adam Smith's Wealth of Nations, p. 17.)

Then, in barter, there is the difficulty of making change. A man who has a horse to sell, and wants a harness, may find a harness maker who wants a horse, but how is the difference in their value to be paid? Then in what terms shall this difference in value be expressed? These difficulties led mankind in primtive times to adopt something that should stand both as a measure and a representative of value. At an early age gold and silver were chosen. Thus, in the days of Abraham, silver money is spoken of as the well known, accepted measure of value, and medium of exchange. "Entreat for me to Ephron, the son of Zohar, that he may give me the cave of Machpelah, which he hath, which is in the end of his field; for as much money as it is worth: he shall give it me for a possession of a burying place amongst you. And Ephron answered Abraham, saying unto him, My Lord hearken unto me: the land is worth four hundred shekels of silver; what is that betwixt me and thee? bury, therefore, thy dead. And Abraham weighed to Ephron the silver which he had named in the audience of the sons of Heth, four hundred shekels of silver, current money with the merchant."—Gen. 23: 9, 15, 16. This was about 1860 years before Christ. So, when an hundred and fifty years later, the sons of Jacob went down to Egypt to buy corn they took MONEY for the purpose.

At present, money is the instrument of commercial transactions among all the trading nations of the earth. But it is only an instrument. Its value depends upon the fact that there are those who may be reached who will accept it in exchange for something that is useful. The solitary survivor of a shipwreck, on an uninhabited, unknown island, who saved a keg of gold coin from the wreck, would have been richer by far, if it had been a keg of nails.

"Money is a machinery for doing quickly and commodiously what would be done, though less quickly and commodiously, without it; and, like many other kinds of machinery, it exerts a distinct and independent influence of its own only when it gets out of order." (Mr. Mill, as quoted by Prof. Walker, in Money, p. 4.)

Gibbon says the early Germans "prized their rude earthen vessels as of equal value with the silver vases, the presents of Rome to their princes and ambassadors. The value of money has been settled by general consent to express our wants and our property, as letters were invented to express our ideas; and both these institutions, by giving a more active energy to the powers and passions of human nature, have contributed to multiply the objects they were designed to represent. The use of gold and silver is in a great measure factitious; but it would be impossible to enumerate the important and various services which agriculture, and all the arts, have received from iron, when tempered and fashioned by the operation of fire and the dexterous hand of man. Money, in a word, is the most universal incitement, iron is the most powerful instrument, of human industry; and it is very difficult to conceive by what means a people neither actuated by the one nor seconded by the other, could emerge from the grossest barbarism." (Rome, v. 1, Chap. 9, p. 260.)

But as the methods of doing business are improved, a system something like the original one of barter, but without its inconveniences is adopted. Thus a Liverpool grain merchant buys a cargo of wheat in New York. About the same time a hardware merchant of New York buys a quantity of cutlery at Sheffield. Instead of incurring the risk and expense of conveying money from Liverpool to New York to pay for the grain, and from New York back to Sheffield to pay for the cutlery, the Liverpool merchant gives for his grain a draft on the Bank of England which the New York merchant buys and sends to pay his bills at Sheffield So between the two countries only the balance of the accounts actually passes in money. In the great money transactions of the day, owing to a carefully devised system of exchanges, but a small portion of the money which enters into the calculations is actually paid. Still, money is at the bottom of these operations, and in the present state of things is as necessary to trade and commerce as are ships and railroads. We should find it difficult to transact the ordinary business of every day life without money.

CHAPTER IV.

WHAT IS MONEY.

THERE is a good deal of literature on the subject of money. But the writers on this subject seem cautious about defining the word money. It is difficult to give a definition that will stand criticism. Perhaps it is sufficient for practical purposes to say that money is an article that will be taken in the final payment of debts, and that will purchase whatever is for sale in the market.

Prof. Jevons says, "Much ingenuity has been spent upon attempts to define the term MONEY, and puzzling questions have arisen as to the precise kind of credit documents which are to be included under the term. Standard legal-tender coin of full weight is undoubtedly money, and as convertible legal tender bank-notes are exactly equivalent to the coined money for which they may at any moment be exchanged, it has often been considered that these also may be included. But inconvertible notes are often made legal tender by law, and can discharge in inland trade all the functions of money. Are they not then to be included?" (Money and Mechanism of Exchange, 248.)

Prof. Walker, (Money, Trade and Industry, p. 4), says:

"Money is that which passes freely from hand to hand throughout the community in final discharge of debts and full payment for commodities, being accepted equally without reference to the character or credit of the person who offers it, and without the intention of the person who receives it, to consume it, or enjoy it, or apply it to any other use than in turn to tender it to others in discharge of debts or payment for commodities."

Dr. Ely, of Johns Hopkins University, says:

"That object is money in the legal sense which is used as money in any case in which the use of money is legally regulated; or whatever is legal tender is money in the legal sense."

Prof. Jevons, with whom in the main, other writers on money agree, describes the functions of money as four:

1. It serves as a medium of exchange. The farmer sells his wheat for money. With his money he buys tools, clothes, groceries, books, whatever he wants. "Money" says Adam Smith, "has become, in all civilized nations, the universal instrument of commerce, by the intervention of which goods of all kinds are bought and sold, or exchanged for one another." (Wealth of Nations, p. 21.)

2. It is used as a common measure of value. Instead of comparing the value of one article with another we express their value in money. We do not say that a horse is worth twenty sheep; but we say of a horse that he is worth a hundred dollars, and of a sheep that it is worth five dollars.

3. Money serves as a standard of value. A farmer going into a new neighborhood wants twenty bushels of wheat to live on. He expects to have wheat to sell in the fall. But he promises to pay—not twenty bushels of wheat—but twenty dollars, the market value of the wheat, with interest. It may

be that fifteen bushels of wheat will pay the debt—it may take thirty. A bushel of wheat will make no more bread at one time than it will at another. Yet it may take more labor to raise a bushel of wheat one year than it does another. If this is the case generally, then, it being scarcer, the price is higher. A bushel of wheat in a bad season represents a greater quantity of labor than it does in a good season. Though money is nominally the standard of value, yet labor, the source of wealth, is the real standard. "At all times and places," says Adam Smith, "that is dear which is difficult to come at, or which it costs much labor to acquire; and that cheap which is to be had easily, or with very little labor. Labor alone, therefore, never varying in its own value, is alone the ultimate and real standard by which the value of all commodities can at all times and places be estimated and compared. It is their real price; money is their nominal price only." (Wealth of Nations, p. 25.)

4. Money serves as a store of value. A man cannot move his farm from New York

to Illinois, but he can put its value in money, in a small bulk, so as easily to transport it and with it buy another wherever he chooses. "At times," says Prof. Jevons, "a person needs to condense his property into the smallest compass, so that he may hoard it away for a time, or carry it with him on a long journey, or transmit to a friend in a distant country. Something which is very valuable, although of little bulk and weight, and which will be recognized as very valuable in every part of the world, is necessary for this purpose. The current money of a country is perhaps more likely to fulfil these conditions than anything else, although diamonds and other precious stones and articles of exceptional beauty and rarity might occasionally be employed." (Money and Mechanism of Exchange, p. 15.)

CHAPTER V.

MATERIAL OF MONEY.

IN new and partly civilized countries different materials have been used as money. "In the rude ages," says Adam Smith, "cattle are said to have been the common instruments of commerce; and, though they must have been a most inconvenient one, yet in old times we find things were frequently valued according to the number of cattle which had been given in exchange for them." (Wealth of Nations, p. 17, 18. A. D. 1776.) "The armour of Diomede," says Homer, "cost only nine oxen; but that of Glaucus cost an hundred oxen. Salt is said to be the common instrument of commerce and exchanges in Abyssinia; a species of shells in some parts of the coast of India; dried cod at Newfoundland; tobacco in Virginia; sugar in some of our West Indian colonies; hides or dressed leather in some other countries; and there is at this day a village in Scotland where it it is not uncommon, I am told, for a workman to carry nails instead of money to the baker shop or the ale house."

Furs and skins were used as money by many ancient nations, and recently by traders with our North American Indians. " Leather money is said to have circulated in Russia as late as the reign of Peter the Great, and it is worthy of notice, that classical writers have recorded traditions to the effect that the earliest currency used at Rome, Lacedaemon and Carthage, was formed of leather." (Money and Mechanism of Exchange, p. 20.)

It is probable that this leather money was representative or token money. The figure of an ox was stamped on leather, and the Shepherd prince who issued it held himself ready to give an ox, on demand, to the person who owned this piece of leather. Hence, the word *pecunia*, from *pecus*, cattle, meant money. From this word is derived our word, *pecuniary*, relating to money. As cattle were reckoned by the head, *capitale*, in Latin, the word *capital* came to mean one's stock in trade. So the word *stock* is used to denote either the domestic animals on a farm, or the shares in an organized company, or in the funded debt of a Government.

Stock is said to be "watered" when the stock which represents a certain property is arbitrarily raised in amount. Thus, when for a railroad which cost thirty millions, stock to the amount of sixty millions was issued, the stock was said to be "watered." The expression originated with a Wall street broker who, before the days of railroads, drove cattle to New York. Dishonest drovers would stop a few miles out of the city and salt their cattle and thus cause them to drink a large quantity of water before they were weighed.

If the people generally will take any thing in payment of debts or in exchange for what they have to sell it answers the purpose of money. "It is," says Prof Walker, "the disposition, or the indisposition, of the great majority of the community to receive it in payment which settles the question whether a particular commodity shall become money or not. The carved pebbles formerly used by the Ethiopians, the wampum which circulated between the New England colonists and the natives, the glass beads used in small payments even down to this day along the Arabian gulf, the shells and the red feathers employed throughout the islands of the Indian ocean, were good money, though serving no other purpose but ornament and decoration, they were desired by the community in general; men would give for them the fruits of their labor, knowing that with them they could obtain most conveniently in turn, in form and amount, the fruits of the labor of others.

"It is in view of its general or universal acceptability that certain writers speak of money as a pledge or security for whatever the holder may wish, now or at a future time to obtain.

"Thus Aristotle, in the ' Nicomachian Ethics,' says: "With regard to a future exchange (if we want nothing at present) money is, as it were our security.

"Mr. McLeod, in the same connection, quotes as follows:

"Boudeau: 'It,' money, 'is a kind of bill

of exchange, or payable at the will of the bearer.'

"Adam Smith: 'A guinea may be considered as a bill for a certain quantity of necessaries or conveniences, upon all the tradesmen of the neighborhood.'

"Thornton: 'Money of every kind is an order for goods.'" (Money, p. 25, 26.)

In modern times, most commercial nations, civilized and semi-civilized, are agreed in taking gold and silver as money.

There are good reasons for this choice of these two metals above all others as *the* material from which to coin money.

1. They have a high market value as bullion among all trading nations. For actual use in daily life neither of them has the intrinsic value of iron. They are not necessary, as material, for the construction of railroads, or for the making of farm or domestic implements, or machinery for factories. Gold and silver are used for works of ornament: iron is a necessity. But both gold and silver have a much higher market value than iron, and on that account, if no other, are a much more suitable material for

money. With iron at four cents a pound it would take one hundred and twenty-five wagon loads of a ton each to buy a farm worth ten thousand dollars.

2. They are sufficiently plenty to furnish material for money and yet sufficiently scarce and difficult to obtain, to prevent their greatly depreciating in value by becoming too plenty.

3. Gold and silver coin will bear a good degree of use in circulation without being so worn by attrition as to lose their weight to that extent that the people will be reluctant to receive them as money. The softer metals would sooner wear out.

4. They are the most beautiful and attractive of all the metals. These are doubtless among the reasons why, by the nations generally, gold and silver are employed as materials for coining money.

Other metals may hereafter come into use.

CHAPTER VI.

GOLD AND SILVER.

THERE is especially in England and Germany a movement, of modern origin, to throw silver out of circulation as money. This movement is doubtless made in the interest of those to whom large sums of money are due. It is the fashion for individuals, corporations, municipalities and nations to go into debt. The national debt of Great Britain was stated to be in 1884, $3,732,149,820; that of Germany, $102,750,000; of France, $3,930,584,845; of the United States $1,830,528,923. Besides this National Debt many of our States are owing large sums. Then nearly every city and village is in debt. Many of the rural towns are bonded, and many farms are mortgaged.

The most of this indebtedness is owing to our citizens. This is also true of Great Britain and France and Germany. This makes a large creditor class. It is composed, for the most part, of intelligent, far sighted members of community. Naturally they are anxious that their money should make as much more money as it honestly can.

In proportion to the scarcity of money the greater is its purchasing power. When money is plenty the price of labor and of property is high. When money is scarce the price of labor and of property is correspondingly low. The less money there is the greater is the purchasing power of a dollar.

For this reason the large creditor class is in favor of contracting the currency, because it would enhance their wealth. This is the reason why silver was demonetized in Germany and in Great Britain. It is the reason why the war against it is waged so persistently in this country. It is for the interest of those to whom debts are owing to have money scarce.

Mr. Seyd estimates that the stock of gold and silver now current as coin, or existing as bullion, is 6,750 millions of dollars, of which 3,250 millions is in silver.

If silver is generally demonetized that will nearly double the value of debts. A dollar would then represent nearly twice the amount of labor and property that it does at present. To pay the debts of local and national governments, taxation would have to be greatly increased, while the ability to pay taxes would be proportionally diminished. The scheme is an ingenious, inhuman one to rob, under the forms of the law, for the benefit of capitalists, the people who must pay the public debts.

In England, silver was legal tender down to the year 1816. The public debt had become great, and at that time the influence of the creditors, who were the capitalists of England, became strikingly apparent. Parliament decreed that gold should be legal-tender in all payments of more than forty shillings.

In Germany gold alone is unlimited legal tender, silver being a legal tender only to a small amount.

In 1873, the Congress of the United States, either through ignorance, or corruption, passed an act demonetizing silver. It is said that the President who signed the bill, did not understand its import. The belief is general that it was passed through the management of the bondholders to multiply the value of their bonds. In consequence of this Act, and of calling in greenbacks, to a large amount, there was great distress throughout the country. Manufacturing, to a great extent, was suspended, workmen could not obtain employment, and in the midst of plenty, people were dying of starvation. Thousands who had been in affluent circumstances were suddenly reduced to poverty. Property mortgaged for one fourth its value when the debt was made, would not sell for enough to pay the mortgage. Able bodied men, by thousands, tramped through the land, seeking in vain for work. At length silver was, by act of Congress, again made legal tender, money became more plenty, and business began to revive.

But avarice is clamorous. At its bidding renewed efforts are being made to degrade silver by stopping its coinage. In violation of the plain provisions of the law, the Treasury Department refuses to use silver in payment of the public debt. At the dictation of the bondholders gold alone is used for this purpose. The financial policy of the Government under the new, as under the old administration is the same in disregarding alike the interests of the people, and their will as expressed by the Laws of the United States.

William of Normandy, with only sixty thousand disciplined soldiers, conquered England full of valiant men. But the English leader, King Harold, was slain in the first battle, the army disorganized and there was nothing left for the undisciplined masses but submission. The bankers and bondholders of this country are comparatively, but a small body, but they are organized and disciplined, and they control, on money matters, the two great parties of the country, and over-ride the interests of the people. They make their influence felt by every Department of the Government. Our law-makers, and our judicial and executive officers are elected by the people. The farmers, unorganized and undisciplined, are overpowered by the money lenders though they greatly out-number them.

Men are blinded by their own interests. Those who have fixed incomes find plausible reasons for diminishing the volume of currency in circulation. But no one will confess that he aims at this. Yet this, says ex-Senator Hill,"was the avowed object of the persons who, under the head of Chevalier, originated, thirty years ago, the plan of employing one and the same metal in all commercial countries. They at first proposed that this metal should be silver, and they actually persuaded some European countries to demonetize gold. They soon, however, changed their tactics, and proposed the demonetization of silver as a more practical method of accomplishing the object of 'abridging the quantity of the circulating medium.'" (N. A. Quarterly, Nov., 1885.)

CHAPTER VII.

SILVER.

SOME recent writers on money, take the position that gold should be the only money of unlimited legal tender. This position is wrong.

That silver, as well as gold, should be used as material for money, is evident from many considerations.

1. There is not enough gold and silver together to form the necessary medium of exchange in the commercial world.

Said Alexander Hamilton, the great financier of Washington's administration: "To annul the use of either of the metals as money is to abridge the quantity of circulating medium, and is liable to all the objections which arise from a comparison of the benefits of a full, with the evils of a scanty circulation." (Report on the Mint.) This observation has far greater weight now than it had when it was made; for the demand for money has increased in greater proportion than the quantity of gold and silver in circulation has increased, notwithstanding the large quantities of both which have been mined within the last half century. Trading nations are still obliged to use a large amount of paper money.

2. Silver has been used as money from the earliest historic ages. In fact, its use from the remotest antiquity has been more general than the use of gold for money. The first mention in history of money is of silver, in the transaction of Abraham, to which reference has already been made.

Herodotus is the oldest of the ancient, profane historians whose works have come down to us. He flourished about 450 years before Christ. In speaking of the great pyramid of Egypt, he says, "On the pyramid is shown an inscription, in Egyptian characters, how much was expended in radishes, onions and garlic for the workmen; which the interpreter, as I well remember, reading the inscription, told me amounted to one thousand six hundred talents of silver." (Carys Herodotus, p. 145.)

Assyria was one of the oldest of nations

Its history has come down to us inscribed in Cuneiform characters on tablets of clay, many of which have recently been discovered. In a history compiled from these monuments, Dr. Smith says, "A husband had the power of divorcing his wife on payment of half a manch of silver." (History of Assyria, p. 14.) This shows that silver was used as money by that ancient nation, probably as long ago as 1120 years before Christ.

A metal which has commended itself to mankind as suitable material for money for over three thousand seven hundred years should not be set aside for the unworthy purpose of making heavier the burdens of debtors.

3. Of the two metals, silver is less liable than gold to large fluctuations in value through a long period of time. The market value of articles of commerce depends largely upon the amount of labor required to produce them. There is far less variation in the amount of labor and capital required to obtain from the mine a given amount of silver than there is to obtain a given amount of gold. Silver is found almost entirely in

the form of ore, combined with other metals. It must be dug, and smelted, and separated from all other substances. To do this always requires labor, and skill, and capital. Gold is often found in large quantities, in the form of dust or flakes, or nuggets, in its pure metallic state, mixed in with ground or sand, from which it is easily separated by washing in water. To do this requires no capital but physical strength, no machines, except a spade and a pan or trough. In this way in 1853 gold was obtained in California to the value of $65,000,000. A common laborer would get from five to fifty dollars a day. Silver is never mined by so simple and inexpensive a method. When these surface, placer diggings, are exhausted, then gold is obtained by getting, often from a great depth, the rock in which it is imbedded, crushing it and separating the gold from the rock and from other minerals. This requires a large capital and a great amount of labor.

4. Again silver is better than gold for money, because it is a harder metal, and therefore can be circulated more without losing in weight and value by abrasion.

For the same reason silver is more useful for domestic purposes, to which use it is applied to a greater extent the more abundant it becomes.

The English, in demonetizing silver, are constantly reproved by the terms they use when speaking or writing of money. For their common denominations of money imply a silver standard.

Adam Smith says, "There were silver coins in England in the time of the Saxons; but there was little gold coined till the time of Edward III., nor any copper till that of James I. of Great Britain. In England, therefore, and for the same reason, I believe, in all other modern nations of Europe, all accounts are kept, and the value of all goods and of all estates, is generally computed in silver, and when we mean to express the amount of a person's fortune, we seldom mention the number of guineas, but the number of pounds sterling which we suppose would be given for it.

"In England gold was not considered as a legal tender for a long time after it was coined into money." (Wealth of Nations, p. 30.)

In speaking of coins, stamped on both sides, he says,

"The denomination of those coins seem originally to have expressed the weight or quantity of metal contained in them.

"The English pound sterling in the time of Edward I. contained a pound, Tower weight, of silver of a known fineness. The Tower pound seems to have been something more than the Roman pound, and something less than the Troyes pound." (Wealth of Nations, p. 20.)

5. The value of money, that is, its purchasing power, will be subject to less variation with a double standard, than if gold alone is used as a standard of value. A sudden shower will raise the water in a mill pond when it will not sensibly affect Lake Erie. So the more money there is in circulation the less will its value be affected by some temporary variation in the amount. The sudden discovery of a rich gold mine is not usually attended by the discovery of silver at the same time.

No two distinct articles of commerce will always have in the market the same relative value. Wheat and corn are in this country staple articles. It costs, in general, twice the labor to produce a bushel of wheat that it does to produce a bushel of corn. But sometimes a bushel of corn sells for as much as a bushel of wheat. But that is no reason why a restriction should be placed upon the raising of either wheat or corn. It can but be in the nature of things that the relative value of gold and silver should vary at times. But this is no reason why the coinage of either into money should be stopped. Yet this is the only reason *assigned* by the mono-metallists for their bitter warfare upon silver coinage in this country.

Germany, by demonetizing silver, has greatly increased the value of the war indemnity which the French are compelled to pay it. England has demonetized silver in the interests of a moneyed aristocracy. The depressing effect upon the common people is seen in the large numbers that emigrate yearly from those countries.

In consequence of the demonetization of

silver in those countries its market value as bullion has fallen. So we are often told what is the market value of our silver dollar, *as bullion*, in those countries. This is done to excite prejudice against it. Why are we not told what is the market value of the nickel, the half dime, or of the copper in the cent, or of the paper on which the bills are printed?

But even in England the metal in their silver or copper coins has not the market value, as bullion, of the face of the coin.

Prof. Jevons says, "The metal contained in a token coin has of course a certain value; but it may be less than the legal value in almost any degree. In our English silver coinage the difference is from nine to twelve per cent. according to the market price of silver; in our bronze coinage the difference is seventy-five per cent. The metal contained in the French bronze coins, is, in like manner, equal in value to little more than one quarter of the current value. In many cases the difference has been far greater as in some of the old kreutzer pieces, lately current in the German States," ("Money" p. 74.)

Though the relative value of gold and silver to each other may vary somewhat, from age to age, owing to the difference in supplies of each of these metals, and to other causes, yet by using both as material for money a closer approximation is made to a permanent and fixed measure of value than would be the case by using one to the exclusion of the other. Heat expands different metals in different degrees. But it is proved that a pendulum composed of several metals will more nearly preserve its length the same in all weathers than one will composed of any one metal.

No two horses can be found of precisely the same weight, and speed, and strength, and power of endurance. Yet an ordinary teamster can draw a greater load with two good horses than with either of them alone. Money, in this commercial age, has railroads and steamboats and costly machinery to build, enormous purchases to make, vast quantities of produce to transport, expensive wars to carry on, and debts to pay of individuals and governments, amounting in the aggregate to enormous sums. Never, in any period of the world's history, was this load as heavy as now; and it would seem the height of madness and of folly where it has heretofore taxed the strength of the two to pull the load, to turn out and dismiss the heavier, steadier and stronger horse of the two, and attempt to move with a one-horse team the burden which the commercial transactions of the day impose on money.

The ratio which the market value of gold and silver bear to each other varies less from age to age than really might be expected.

Herodotus, speaking of the tribute that was paid to Darius, said that "gold was estimated at thirteen times the value of silver." (History, p. 212.)

At present the ratio of gold to silver, as established by law, in this country, is 16 to 1. In France it is 15.5 to 1. The difference between their relative value now and twenty-four hundred years ago is not sufficiently great to be alarming.

The quantity of gold and silver in the markets of the world gradually increases as new mines are discovered. In ten years after the discovery of gold in California, in the year 1848, as much gold was produced as had been in the previous 356 years.

British America and Australia gave large contributions to the world's store of the precious metals.

Commercial nations were greatly alarmed at this sudden influx of gold. They supposed that it would suffer a great depreciation in value. Says Prof. Levi, "Frightened, and not without reason, at the possible consequences, some countries, heretofore anxious to attract and retain gold in circulation, even at great sacrifices, showed a feverish anxiety to banish it altogether. In July, 1850, Holland demonetized the gold ten dollar piece and the Guillaume. Portugal prohibited any gold from having a current value, except English sovereigns. Belgium demonetized its gold circulation, Russia prohibited the export of silver; and France, alarmed, but less hasty, issued a commission to inquire into the matter." (Hist. British Commerce, p. 336.)

Yet these fearful forebodings were not realized. No sensible harm has resulted from the great quantities of gold and silver, which in modern times have been discovered and put upon the market. There are enough poor people in the world, who can use for procuring the comforts of life all the gold and silver which they can obtain by honest industry.

Both should be kept in circulation. The efforts making to degrade silver do not appear to be in the interests of humanity.

The impression is sought to be made that silver is not used as money by commercial nations generally. This is a great mistake. The Bank of France alone holds over seventeen millions of dollars more in silver than the United States ever coined. The people probably hold half as much more. Her silver is a full legal tender. Yet it does not drive the gold out of the country. All the continental nations of Europe, except Germany, make silver a legal tender. It is the money chiefly used in India, Japan and China.

"The English government," says Prof. Jevons, "has repeatedly tried to introduce a gold currency into our Indian possessions, but has always failed, and the gold coins now circulating there are supposed not to exceed one tenth part of the metallic currency. Although the pouring out of forty or fifty millions sterling of silver from Germany may for some years depress the price of the metal, it can be gradually absorbed without difficulty by the Eastern nations, which have for two or three thousand years received a continual stream of the precious metals from Europe. If other nations should one after another demonetize silver, yet the East may be found quite able to absorb all that is thrust upon it, provided that this be not done too rapidly." (Money, p. 142.)

Those who in this country are carrying on the war against the farther coinage of silver make the impression that silver is so much more plenty than gold that there is danger that silver will supplant gold, and that our metallic money will be chiefly silver. This idea is often presented, and many have come to believe that it is true. But it is utterly false. There is no undue proportion of silver in the country.

During the fiscal year ending June 30th,

1885, the value of the gold deposited at the mints and assay offices of the United States was $56,748,752.60. The value of the silver so deposited during the same period was $38,082,222.87. (Report of the Director of the Mint, p. 3, 4.)

Here we see that the excess of gold over silver brought to our mints the last year was $18,666,529.73, or almost 50 per cent.

But it is claimed that, because England and Germany have demonetized silver, and silver has, in consequence depreciated somewhat in market value as bullion, that "the poorer money will drive out the better," and the gold be carried out of the country, and the silver from those countries be brought in to displace it.

But this is also disproved by the facts. From the same authority we learn that the imports of silver into the United States were —for the fiscal year above referred to—of bullion to the value of $4,530,384; of coin, $12,020;243, of which $673,926 were our own coin. This makes a total of silver imported for the year, $16,550,627. During the same period gold was imported to the value of, in bullion, $11,221,846.45; in coin, $17,842,459. Total, $29,063,305.45. (Ibid.) So that notwithstanding all these predictions, there were imported into the country during the last fiscal year, $12,512,678.45 more gold than silver!

But this does not probably represent the whole truth; for the imports of silver are given from the books of the Custom houses—though much of it did not go to the mints—but only that amount of gold imported is given above which was deposited at the mints and assay offices.

The exports of silver for the same period were — of bullion $20,422,924—of American coin, $1,211,627--Foreign silver coin, $12,060,612. Total export of silver $33,695,163.

The exports of gold were, of bullion, $395,750; of American coin, $2,345,809. Foreign gold coin, $5,736,333. Total exports of gold; $8,477,892. This shows that the value of silver exported for the year exceeded the value of the gold exported by $25,216,671. This shows that the accumulation of gold over silver in the country during the last fiscal year has been over 300 per cent.

It seems incredible that, in the face of these facts, intelligent men can raise such a clamor against silver coinage!

Dwell upon these figures until you become familiar with the true story which they tell. You will then see that if there could be such a thing, we should be in much more danger of a glut of gold than of silver.

The Director of the Mint estimates the amount of coin in this country, July 1st, 1885, at $820,000,000; of which, $542,000,000 consisted of gold coin, and $278,000,000 of silver coin. (Ibid, p. 27.)

It is objected that the silver does not go into general circulation.

To this we reply that there is more silver in circulation among the people than there is gold.

"The number of silver dollars coined under the provisons of the act of February 28, 1878, amounted to $213,259,431 on November 1st, 1885, of which $163,817,342 remained in the Treasury of the United States, while $49,442,089 were in circulation on that date." (Report of the Comptroller of the Currency, p. 18.)

Why does so large an amount of silver remain in the Treasury?

It is simply because the paper which represents it is lighter to carry and easier to count.

The next paragraph in the Report says that "Silver certificates have been issued, which are represented by standard silver dollars in the Treasury of the United States, to the amount of $125,053,286." If silver certificates are in circulation it is the same as if the silver was in circulation. Of these certificates $31,906,514 have, in the course of business found their way back to the Treasury.

It would also add to the circulation of silver if the Treasurer would use the silver received for duties, to pay the interest and principal on United States Bonds, as he is required to do by law.

The moneyd power has already become so strong that it overrides the laws. This silver is kept hoarded contrary to law, and the officials who do it, complain that it is not in circulation, and ask to have silver coinage stopped on that account!

Remember that, according to the official reports of the government there was during the last fiscal year.

1. More gold than silver brought to the mints and assay offices of the U. S. Government.

2. More gold than silver imported into the country.

3. More silver than gold exported from the country.

So that relatively over three hundred per cent. more gold than silver was in the year past being accumulated in this country.

In the light of these facts there does not seem to be but one explanation of the outcry made against silver coinage and that is that this outcry is made in the interests of the bondholders without regard to the welfare of the country as a whole.

CHAPTER VIII.

PAPER MONEY.

THOUGH gold and silver be both used as material for money, yet the quantity of those which any commercial nation can keep in circulation is insufficient to meet the demands of trade. Hence the necessity for paper money. In commercial centers, checks, bills of exchange, and other representatives of value, are made to do the work of money. In the Clearing Houses of New York and London, by means of which the accounts between banks are settled, an immense business is transacted daily with the use of but very little money. Balances only are paid and they generally by checks.

Paper is lso used as a substitute for metallic money for its greater convenience. To carry about a few thousand dollars in gold would be a burden; but a hundred, five hundred, or thousand dollar bills would not be inconvenient to carry, and the same amount in a draft would not be noticed. Hence, no matter how plenty metallic money is, extensive business transactions require the use of paper in some form as a substitute.

In some other respects paper money has the advantage over metallic. Gold and silver suffer abrasion and consequently lose in value by daily use. In time, this money becomes so worn and light, that people are unwilling to take it, and difficulty, and sometimes great national distress results.

It is also liable to mutilation by boring, and sweating, and other processes by which a part of the metal is abstracted, while the coin presents the appearance of being simply worn by use. In England, before the art of coining money was brought to its present state of perfection, their coins were mutilated by clippings and parings, as well as worn by use, until the current money lost nearly half its value. To put a stop to mutilating the coin, the severest penalties were inflicted. Macaulay says, (History of England, p. 87, *et seq.*). "It is to no purpose that the rigorous laws against coining and clipping were rigorously executed. At every session that was held at the Old Baily, terrible examples were made. Hurdles, with four, five, or six wretches convicted of counterfeiting, or mutilating the money of the realm, were dragged, month after month, up Holborn Hill. One morning seven men were hanged, and a woman burned for clipping. But all was in vain.

"The evil proceeded with constantly accelerating velocity. At length in the autumn of 1695 it could hardly be said that the country possessed, for practical purposes, any measure of the value of commodities. It was a mere chance whether what was called a shilling was really ten pence, six pence or a groat.

"The results of some experiments which were tried at that time, deserve to be mentioned.

"Three eminent London goldsmiths were invited to send a hundred pounds each in current silver to be tried by the balance. Three hundred pounds ought to have weighed about twelve hundred ounces. The actual weight proved to be six hundred and twenty-four ounces.

"The evils produced by this state of the currency were not such as have generally been thought worthy to occupy a prominent place in history. Yet it may well be doubted whether all the misery which had been inflicted on the English nation, in a quarter of a century, by bad kings, bad ministers, bad parliaments, and bad judges, was equal to the misery caused in a single year by bad crowns and bad shillings. Those events which furnish the best themes for pathetic or indignant eloquence are not always those which most affect the happiness of the great body of the people. The misgovernment of Charles and James, gross as it had been, had not prevented the common business of life from going steadily and prosperously on. While the honor and independence of the state was sold to a foreign power, while chartered rights were invaded, while fundamental laws were violated, hundreds of thousands of quiet, honest, and industrious families labored and traded, ate their meals and lay down to rest, in comfort and security.

But when the great instrument of exchange became thoroughly deranged, all trades, all industries were smitten as with a palsy. The evil was felt daily and hourly in most every class; in the dairy and on the threshing floor, by the anvil and the loom, on the billows of the ocean, and in the depths of the mine. Nothing could be purchased without a dispute. Over every counter there was wrangling from morning to night. The workman and his employer had a quarrel as regularly as the Saturday came around. On a fair day, or a market day, the clamors, the reproaches, the taunts, the curses were incessant, and it was well if no booth was overturned and no head broken. No merchant would contract to deliver goods without making some stipulation about the quality of the coin in which he was to be paid. Even men of business were often bewildered by the confusion into which all pecuniary transactions were thrown. The simple and the careless were pillaged without mercy by extortioners whose demands grew even more rapidly than the money shrank. The price of the necessaries of life rose fast. The laborer found that the bit of metal, which, when he received it, was called a shilling, would hardly when he wanted to purchase a loaf of bread, go as far as sixpence.

Where artisans of more than usual intelligence were collected in great numbers, as in the dockyard at Chatham, they were able to make their complaints heard and to obtain some redress. But the ignorant and helpless peasant was cruelly ground between one class which would give money only by tale and another which would take it only by weight.

"To remedy these evils the Recoinage Act was passed. The debased coins were melted and recoined at an expencse to the country of one million two hundred thousand pounds sterling."

Coins made of gold and silver, durable as they are, yet when constantly used, even in a legitimate manner, undergo a loss which in a few years sensibly detracts from their value.

Speaking of the present gold coins of England, Prof. Jevons, says, "A large part of the gold coinage is worn below the least current weight, and all persons of experience avoid paying old sovereigns to the Bank of England.

Only ignorant and unlucky persons, or else larger banks and companies which cannot otherwise get rid of light coin, suffer loss. The quantity of light gold coin withdrawn by the banks did not for many years exceed half a million a year; during the last few years it has varied from £700,000 to £950,000. As the average amount of gold coined annually is four or five millions, and the coins melted or exported are for the most part new and of full weight, it follows necessarily, that the currency is becoming more and more deficient in weight."

There is great injustice in making the loss in the weight of gold coins which have been in use for thirty or forty years fall upon the last holder. The mint should take all light coins at their nominal value and replace them by coins of full weight. Still the loss resulting from the use of coin money is a total one, though borne, as it should be by the people at large.

Paper money has this advantage over metallic money that it can be replaced when worn by use, with but trifling expense.

Another advantage is that large amounts

are more readily counted. A New York daily paper, in reporting the business of the Clearing House of that city for that day says that its exchanges amounted to $116,747,578: the balances to $4,551,297. This amount of business is not spoken of as exceptionally large. It would be simply impossible to do it in a single institution if in each transaction gold and silver were actually paid.

If paper money can be made perfectly safe, without a possibility of losing its value either in whole or in part, it will be generally preferred in common use to gold or silver.

The preference which the people have for paper money if perfectly safe is seen by a fact stated by the United States Treasurer in his recent report. He says, page 14, "The issue of silver cirtificates, by treasury officers in the South and West, for gold coin deposited with the assistant treasurer at New York, under departmental circular of September 18, 1880, was discontinued in January last (1885). The amount which had been issued in this manner to the date named was $80,730,500."

Gold coin was paid for these *silver certificates*, redeemable only in silver, simply because the people prefer good paper money to the very best metallic money.

But paper money should be MONEY, and not a promise to pay money. The money of a country, gold and silver and paper, should be interconvertible; but neither kind should be redeemable. Payment in any kind of money should be final.

CHAPTER IX.
COINING MONEY.

THE money of any nation should be a legal tender for debts in every part of that nation. It should carry its full nominal value with it wherever it goes. But this is not likely to be the case unless the government creates the money.

The power to control the money of a nation carries with it almost every other power. The money power is well nigh supreme. Hence, the right to coin money is vested in the Supreme Power of the State. It is a maxim of the civil law that *monelandi jus principum ossibus inhæret.* "The right of coining money inheres in the bones of princes." In all monarchical countries this right is jealously guarded as the prerogative of the Crown.

Says Prof. F. A. Walker, "In all lands coinage has been one of the most cherished prerogatives of sovereignty." (Money, p. 168.)

Our constitution vests in Congress the right to coin money. No state, however far it may have pushed its theories of "State Rights," has ever ventured to claim in words this fundamental prerogative of sovereignty. This right of the National Government remains unchallenged.

If the National Government has the exclusive right to coin money, then it should furnish the money for the use of the people, no matter of what material it is made. If a substitute for gold and silver is permitted, then the government should furnish the substitute. This is evident. A prerogative can be of but little value if it may be easily supplanted.

Yet, up to the period of our civil war, the bulk of the money in use in this country was furnished by banks chartered by the several states. This was a strange inconsistency. It was a great annoyance and detriment to the people. The money current in one State was not good in another. The money of Illinois would not buy a dinner in

New York. Many of the banks were worthless. A general bank failure occurred every few years.

Thomas Jefferson said of the bank suspension of 1814, "The banks have pronounced their own sentence of death. Between two and three hundred millions of dollars of their promissory notes are in the hands of the people for solid produce and property sold, and they formally declare they will not pay them. * *

"Thus by the dupery of our citizens, and tame acquiescence of our legislators, the nation is plundered of two or three hundred millions of dollars, treble the amount of debt contracted in the revolutionary war, and which, instead of redeeming our liberty, has been expended on sumptuous houses, carriages and dinners. A fearful tax if equalized on all, but overwhelming and convulsive by its partial fall." (Jefferson's Works, vol. 6, p. 295.)

That all the money, paper as well as metallic, needed by the country should be issued by the National Government directly, we urge from the following considerations:

1. Congress is exclusively empowered by the Constitution to do it.

Our best writers on constitutional law agree that the phrase "To coin money" applies to paper as well as metallic money.

Judge Farrar, in his "Manual of the Constitution," §568, says:

"Congress is not restricted as to the materials they may make use of, or their worth or value, independent of their authorized use as money; nor is it required that they should have any such value. Even the operation of converting them into money is described only by the verb 'to coin,' which, if it means anything in addition to the act of converting it into money, includes only the Government stamp, by which the act is authenticated."

Daniel Webster (Works, vol. 4. p. 315), says:

"It is clear that the power to regulate commerce among the states carries with it, not impliedly, but necessarily and directly, a full power of regulating the essential element of commerce, namely, the currency of the country, the money which constitutes the life and soul of commerce."

In his "Money and the Mechanism of Exchange," p. 317, ad sequitur, Professor Jevons says:

"The issue of notes is more analagous to the royal function of coinage than to the ordinary commercial operation of drawing bills. We ought to talk of COINING NOTES, as John Law did; fo though the design is impressed on paper instead of metal, the function of the note is exactly the same as that of a representative token. As to the right to issue promises, it no more exists than the right to establish private mints. As almost every one has long agreed to place the coinage of money in the hands of the Executive Government, so I believe that the issue of paper, representative money should continue to be practically in the hands of the Government, or its agents acting under the strictest legislative control."

It would be less absurd and less dangerous to permit private individuals, or corporations to coin metallic money than to permit them to issue paper money. But the Constitution in prohibiting the one prohibits the other.

2. Paper money issued by the National Government in a properly limited amount would be of permanent value. It would rest upon a real basis—the entire resources of the country. Paper money issued upon what is called a "gold basis," rests upon a *fictitious* basis. The banks do not have gold in their vaults to the value of the bills they issue. If they did, why issue the bills? Why not put the gold in circulation? But the banks formerly issued at least three times as much paper money as they had coin with which to redeem it. Said a bank president, holding out a bill, "We here promise to pay five dollars, but there is the tacit proviso, *if we are not called upon to pay it*. If the payment of all our bills is demanded we can but suspend."

Our National Bank Bills are good simply because they rest upon the credit of the Government; they are redeemable in legal tenders issued by the Government.

The Banks do not indorse their bills. They are, therefore, no better than if issued directly by the Government.

3. It would be a great saving to the country if all the bills now issued by the National Banks were issued by the Government. These bills are secured by Government bonds. On these bonds interest is paid. The amount that has already been thus taken from the tax-payers and given to the rich is enormous. This drain from the pockets of the people into the pockets of rich capitalists should be stopped. The Government should, as rapidly as possible, pay these bonds and issue all the paper money directly. Let the people at large be the creditors of the Government.

The total amount of bonds held by the National Banks November 1st, 1885, was, according to the Report of the Comptroller of the Currency, $308,364,550. (Report, p. 70.) "The average rate of interest now paid by the United States on the bonds deposited as security for circulating notes is a little more than .036 per cent. upon their par value." (Report; p. 32.) The rate of interest formerly paid to the banks was 6 per cent. But even at the reduced rate, the amount of interest now yearly paid by the Government to the National Banks is a large sum.

For every hundred thousand dollars in bonds that a bank deposits with the Government, it gives the bank ninety thousand dollars. The Government pays the banks interest on the bonds; but the banks do not pay the Government any interest on this money. The interest donated by the Government to the National Banks for the year 1885 amounted to $10,590,011.42. If this large sum was donated yearly to the poor families who are struggling with hardships on the frontier to make themselves homes, we would not complain. But it is given, without any just reason, to the rich.

But not only would the interest be saved, if the Government issued all the paper money, but much of the principal. Every year a large amount in bills is destroyed by fire and flood and other accidents. The loser would be the individual, the tax-payers would be the gainers. We may form some opinion as to what this would amount to in the aggregate from a single circumstance. During the war, the Government issued fractional currency to the amount of 45 millions of dollars. When called in, but 30 millions were presented. The people gained 15 millions of dollars by this one transaction.

4. It would add greatly to the prosperity of the country to release, for industrial purposes, the capital now tied up by the National Banks in Government bonds. The resources of this country, to a great extent, are yet undeveloped. There are plenty of men willing to work but no man hires them. The capitalist, who should set the unemployed to building and manning ships, and railroads, and working mines and farms and factories, spends at his office an hour or two a day examining securities, reckoning his interest, and cutting off his coupons. Set the three hundred and eight millions now lying idle in Government bonds at work in legitimate, useful enterprises, and it would do a vast amount of good. It would give a mighty impetus to business to unloose this large amount of capital so that it could be employed in productive industries. It would make many homes comfortable that are now destitute. It would increase im-

mensely the wealth of the country, by encouraging labor, the only source of wealth.

5. No self-constituted body of men should have, under a republican form of government, the power to control the business interests of the country, so as to make them at their own will, prosperous or adverse. No matter how respectable may be this body; no matter how wisely, on the whole, they may use this power; it is too dangerous for any but the people at large to wield.

But the National Banks possess this power. They can make every branch of business lively by inflating the currency. They can clog and stop the wheels of industry by contracting the currency.

There is no legal limit to their power to inflate the currency; or, on the other hand, to contract it.

One year, business may be prosperous, prices good, labor in demand. Every body is encouraged to enlarge his business facilities, and to go in debt, and to make ventures. Then the banks may contract, call in their money, refuse accommodations; and bankruptcy and misery follow. This power, to a limited extent, was exercised in Jefferson's day. Respecting it he says,

"It is cruel that such revolutions in private fortunes should be at the mercy of avaricious adventurers, who, instead of employing their capital, if any they have, in manufactures, commerce, and other useful pursuits, make it an instrument to burthen all the interchanges of property with their swindling profits, profits which are the price of no useful industry of theirs." (Jefferson's Works, vol. 6, p. 296.)

Again he says, (Works, vol. 7, p. 64),

"The bank mania is raising up a moneyed aristocracy in our country which has already set the government at defiance, and although forced at length to yield a little on the first essay of their strength, their principles are unyielded and unyielding. These have taken deep root in the hearts of that class from which our legislators are drawn, and the sop to Cerberus, from fable has become history. Their principles lay hold of the good, their pelf of the bad, and thus those whom the constitution had placed as guards to its portals are sophisticated or suborned from their duties."

It must be borne in mind that for men to obtain this power, the one qualification is, the possession of money. No matter how they obtained their money, or what is their character. If ten men buy a hundred thousand dollars worth of Government bonds, they can obtain a charter for a National Bank. The Government will give them ninety thousand dollars in bills, *without interest*, hold their bonds for the redemption of these bills, and yet *pay them interest on the bonds.* These bills they can loan out on interest to business men. Or they can add ten thousand dollars to the money received from the Government and again buy bonds and obtain the charter for another bank. This operation, it was said, was repeated ten times by certain parties when the National Bank Act first became a law. With less than two hundred thousand dollars invested they drew from the Government interest on one million of dollars! And they did nothing contrary to law.

The National Banks can expand or contract at pleasure, the currency they issue. In point of fact they have (Report of the Comptroller of the Currency, p. 14) contracted their circulation the last three years $48,000,154.

6. The objection so often made, that bills issued by the Government are "fiat money" has not in it the slightest force whatever. It is a ridiculous attempt to frighten the people with a harmless bugbear. A "fiat" is a decree or command. All money is "fiat money." That is, it is constituted money by the decree of the Government.

The material of which it is made has nothing to do with it. Gold of the finest quality is not money until it is made into money by the Government. Men may buy it as a commodity, but no one is obliged to take it for a debt. But let the Government coin it, and stamp it as money, and it becomes money.

It passes now everywhere in the Nation for the sum stamped upon it. Before it was made into coin it had a market value, as metal, but *it was not money*. No one was obliged to take it. Whatever is legal tender is made so by civil authority. It is "fiat money."

Our gold coins are not current in England. They are bought, like iron and steel, by weight, at market value. Our metallic money is there a commodity. Bullion is gold or silver uncoined—usually in bars.

"Within a country," says Bagehot, "the action of a Government can settle the quantity and therefore the value of its currency, but outside its own country no Government can do so. Bullion is the 'cash' of international trade; paper currencies are of no use there, and coins pass only as they contain more or less bullion." (Lombard Street, p. 44.)

The Revised Statutes of the United States, Sec. 3,588, say, "United States notes shall be lawful money and a legal tender in payment of all debts public and private, within the United States, except for duties on imports and interest on the public debt."

Thus the law declares that United States notes shall be—not the representative of money—not a demand for money—but money itself—*lawful money.* And this money was

COINING MONEY.

to be good for all purposes for which money could be used, with a single, specified exception.

This exception was a great mistake. But for that, these notes would not have depreciated as they did. The National debt could have been paid and the Nation saved an untold amount of misery.

All money, then, should be issued by the Government. The power to issue paper money should be taken from private corporations and placed in the hands of the Representatives of the people, where by right and by the Constitution it belongs.

CHAPTER X.

BASIS OF PAPER MONEY.

WE have shown in brief that the basis of paper money is *actual property*, and not *imaginary* gold and silver. But there is so much misapprehension on this subject that it needs a farther elucidation.

The money issued by our National Banks is better than that formerly issued by the State Banks, for this reason; the State Banks *promised* to pay the amount represented by their bills in current *coin*; when they did not have, never had, and never expected to have sufficient coin to pay their notes in circulation. When the call to pay was generally made they met it by suspension. They sometimes paid from ten to fifty cents on the dollar; and sometimes nothing. Their circulation rested on an *imaginary* basis.

The National Banks do not promise to pay in coin; but in United States *legal tenders*. Hence their bills are as good as the

BASIS OF PAPER MONEY.

legal tenders of the United States Government, but no better. If the banks fail, the depositors suffer, but the bills remain good. They rest on a solid basis—on the credit of the government of a country, rich in its resources and in the general industry and thrift of its inhabitants.

It is remarkable, that the only paper money that has never depreciated is that which has been issued by Governments to meet an exigency, with no definite promise to pay, either on demand or at any stated time.

Venice was founded on seventy or eighty islets in a lagoon on the northwest fringe of the Adriatic Sea, by refugees from the Huns, when they ravaged Italy A. D. 452. It soon rose to importance, and for many years was one of the first commercial cities in Europe.

In the year 1171 the Venetian republic (Abridged from "The Money Question" by Wm. A. Berkey. See also N. A. R. Sept. 1885, p. 205.) being engaged in expensive wars, made forced loans upon its wealthiest citizens, on which loans it agreed to pay four per cent interest per annum. A chamber of loans was organized and the creditors made the managers. Each one was credited on the books the amount of his loan. These loans were transferable on the books, either in whole or in part. This institution naturally grew into a bank.

It was soon found that to pay debts of large amounts by a transfer of a loan on the books was much more easily and safely done than by carrying and counting coin. Hence, after the Republic ceased to want money, merchants and others deposited coin and secured credits. The transfers were made so frequently that no one cared for the interest, and the government ceased to pay interest.

In the year 1423 it was decreed that all bills of exchange payable in Venice should be paid in this bank unless otherwise stipulated. This added greatly to its business. Its paper was generally at a premium, often so great that the premium was limited by law to 20 per cent.

Though established at so early a period, when society was unsettled, and the subject of finance was so little understood, this bank never suspended, nor failed. During the 600 years of its existence there was never a money panic at Venice. Its credits remained good until the Venetian Republic was overthrown in the wars of Napoleon.

The Bank of England was also created to meet the necessities of the Government. Charles II. committed a great crime and blunder. "The goldsmiths of London," says Walter Bagehot, "who then carried on upon a trifling scale what we should now call banking, used to deposit their reserve of treasure in the 'Exchequer,' with the sanction and under the care of the Government. In many European countries the credit of the State had been so much better than any other credit, that it had been used to strengthen the beginnings of banking. The honesty of the English Government was trusted implicitly. But Charles II. showed that it was trusted undeservedly. He shut up the 'Exchequer,' would pay no one, and so the goldsmiths were ruined.

The credit of the Stuart Government never recovered from this monstrous robbery, and the Government created by the Revolution of 1688 could hardly expect to be more trusted with money than its predecessor. A government created by a revolution hardly ever is.". (Lombard Street p. 93.)

In 1694, the credit of the Government of William III. was so low in London that it was impossible for it to borrow any large sum.

The Government was in the greatest financial straits. At last they hit upon a scheme to relieve their pressing necessities.

"The plan," says Macaulay, "was that twelve hundred thousand pounds should be raised at what was then considered the moderate rate of 8 per cent. interest. In order to induce the subscribers to advance the money promptly on terms so unfavorable to the public, the subscribers were to be incorporated by the name of the Governor and Company of the Bank of England. They were so incorporated and then £1,200,000 was obtained." (Lombard Street p. 94.)

This was the beginning of the English National Debt.

To this Bank were granted several important privileges.

1. It was to be the sole depository of the Government funds.

2. It was the only bank in which the stockholders were not personally liable for its debts.

3. It had the privilege of being the *sole joint stock company* permitted to issue bank notes in England.

These bank notes were to be redeemable in coin.

In times of panic the Bank suspended cash payments. At one time the suspension lasted 22 years, from 1797 to 1819.

In 1844, the Bank of England was re-organized. The Bank was authorized to issue bills to the amount of fifteen million pounds sterling secured by Government bonds in its possession, *without being obliged to redeem these bills in coin.* All notes that it issued above this amount were to be secured by gold and silver coin and bullion in its vaults. In consequence of this arrangement it has not again suspended. It has passed through several panics since, but has not been obliged to suspend specie payments on that part of its circulation which it was under obligation to pay in coin. So large a portion of its circulation is secured by the credit of the Government that the Bank is able to keep the rest good under all circumstances.

We see then from these instructive examples that the proper basis for paper money is the credit of the Government—that is the property, the business, and the resources of the entire country.

Our National Bank bills rest upon this basis, and, therefore, they are better than any paper money this country ever had, except the greenbacks which they, to an extent supplanted, which rest upon the same basis.

But there is the objection to the issuing of paper money by the National Banks which we have already mentioned. The Government *gives* these Banks *the use, without interest*, of all the notes they have in circulation.

The National Banks pay a tax of one-half of one per cent. on their circulation, and this is the only offset they make for the free use of the money furnished them by the Government. The proceeds of this tax are used to pay the cost of printing the bills and other expenses incident to the furnishing of these bills by the Government.

The objection is sometimes made to paper money that it has but little intrinsic value. The same objection might be made to an ordinary deed. But it conveys a title to that which has value.

Properly speaking, the intrinsic value of any thing to man, is the value that inheres in the thing itself. The intrinsic value of food to a starving man is the same whether it costs little or much.

The market value of any thing is the price which it will bring. Iron, in itself considered, is of much more value to man than gold or silver. We could not very well keep house without iron. But its abundance, and the ease with which it is obtained makes it cheap. When a savage who had never heard of gold or money, was offered by Captain Cook, a guinea, or a handful of nails, for provisions, he wisely chose the latter. They had the greater intrinsic value.

CHAPTER XI.

BANKS.

IN the modern mode of conducting business, banks are a necessity. But the issuing of money is no necessary part of banking. Some of the best banks have never had a bill of their own issue in circulation. It would be about as proper for a farm to issue money as for a bank to issue money.

Referring to the bank of England, Prof. F. A. Walker says, "The greatest bank in the world is not, as a bank, an issuer of notes, a manufacturer of paper money. Nor are the joint stock banks of London, with their enormous deposits and discounts dependent in the smallest degree for their power or their profits on note circulation. No London bank can issue notes, nor can any bank which has been chartered since May 6, 1844, while the issues of the English banks then existing are limited to their ordinary outstanding circulation before that date." (Money p. 449.)

Among the proper functions of a bank are these: 1. To receive deposits. The capital of a bank is not needed so much to carry on its business as to inspire public confidence. People who have confidence in the bank, deposit their money with it for safe keeping, and that usually for short periods, subject to being paid whenever called for. This money the bank lends on short loans. "Thus a banker's business—his proper business"—says Walter Bagehot—"does not begin while he is using his own money; it commences when he begins to use the capital of others." (Lombard Street. p. 244.)

2. To make discounts, or loans, on good security and for a short time. The same men who deposit money with the bank, subject to call, that is, loan it to the bank, frequently have occasion to borrow of the bank. But all who deposit money do not do it at the same time, and all who borrow do not borrow at the same time. Money is being paid out and paid in to the bank all the time, and these

amounts generally very nearly balance each other.

3. To exchange—that is to receive money at the bank and pay it out in a distant, or even foreign city. Usually, banks have funds on deposit at a convenient business metropolis for this purpose.

Banks do not need subsidies from the Government any more than mills or stores or farms. Wherever a bank is really needed, a bank will be established. The demand will bring a supply. Men of means will enter upon the business of banking as they do upon any other kind of business—to make money. For, apart from issuing bills, banking, when properly conducted, is profitable business. In speaking of joint stock companies, Walter Bagehot says, "As a rule, the most profitable of these companies are banks.

Indeed, *all* the favoring conditions concur in many banks. An old, established bank has a 'prestige' which amounts to a 'privileged opportunity;' though no exclusive right is given to it by law, a peculiar power is given to it by opinion. The business of banking ought to be simple; if it is *hard* it is *wrong*.

The only securities which a banker, using money that he may be asked at short notice to repay, ought to touch, are those which are easily saleable and easily intelligible. If there is a difficulty or a doubt, the security should be declined. No business can of course be quite reduced to fixed rules. There must be occasional cases which no preconceived theory can define. But banking comes as near to fixed rules certainly as any existing business, perhaps as any possible business. The business of an old, established bank has the full advantage of being a simple business, and in part the advantage of being a monopoly business. Competition with it is only open in the sense in which competition with "the London Tavern" is open; any one that has to do with either will pay dear for it.

But the main source of the profitableness of established banking is the smallness of the requisite capital. Being only wanted as a "moral influence," it need not be more than is necessary to secure that influence. Although, therefore, a banker deals only with the most sure securities, and with those which yield the least interest, he can, nevertheless, gain and divide a very large profit upon his own capital, because the money in his hands is so much larger than that capital.

Experience, as shown by plain figures, confirms these conclusions." (Lombard Street. p. 244. *et seq.*)

He then gives the respective profits of 110 banks in England, Scotland and Ireland. These banks pay dividends as follows:

 15 banks pay above 20 per cent.
 20 " " between 15 and 20 per cent.
 36 " " " 10 " 15 "
 36 " " " 5 " 10 "
 3 only pay less than 5 per cent.

"That is to say, above 25 per cent of the capital employed in these banks pays over 15 per cent, and 62 1-2 per cent of the capital pays more than 10 per cent. So striking a result is not to be shown in any other joint stock trade.

"The period to which these accounts refer was certainly not a particularly profitable one—on the contrary, it has been specially unprofitable. The rate of interest has been very low, and the amount of good security in the market is small. Many banks—to some extent most banks—probably had in their books painful reminiscences of 1866. The fever of excitement which passed over the nation was strongest in the classes to whom banks lent most, and consequently the losses of even the most careful banks (save of those in rural and sheltered situation) were probably greater than usual. But even tried by this very unfavorable test banking is a trade profitable far beyond the average of trades."

These remarks, coming from a high financial authority, are made respecting banks in countries, the resources of which are well developed. Money cannot be used to the advantage that it can in this country. There is not the demand for it that there is here, nor can they afford to pay the same rate of interest.

Then, to have banks, it is not necessary to have "National Banks." It is not necessary that the use of the capital of these banks shall be furnished by the Government, free of interest. Let those who engage in the banking business furnish their own capital.

Some have done so all along.

We give a sketch, kindly furnished us by the cashier of the Chemical Bank of New York, Wm. J. Quinlan, Jr.:

"The Chemical Manufacturing Co. was chartered, in 1824, with the privilege of banking. The charter expired in 1844, when the Chemical Bank was organized, with a capital of $300,000. On January 1st, 1849, the first dividend was paid, being 6 per cent., the surplus then amounting to about $200,000. A yearly dividend of 12 per cent. was paid for several years, which was then increased to 18 per cent. per annum; in a few years the dividend was increased to 24 per cent. per annum; again, to 36 per cent.; again, to 60 per cent., and in 1872 the dividend was made 100 per cent. per annum, and has continued at that rate to the present time. All the accumulations have been earned since 1844.

The bank became the "Chemical National Bank of New York" in 1865, under the provision of Congress, allowing State organizations to enter the National system.

The Chemical Bank issued currency, and

there is about $10,000 yet outstanding. The Chemical National Bank never issued any bills.

The bank has never suspended.

The *par* value of each share is $100. The bid price is $2,800 to $2,900, for each share, but it is rarely offered for sale, excepting when an estate is closed.

Dividends paid since 1844, in round numbers, $6,000,000.

Our success is largely due to the able management of Mr. John Q. Jones, who was President from 1844 to his death, 1878, and to that of our present President, Geo. G. Williams, who was Cashier from 1855 to 1878, and who succeeded Mr. Jones to the Presidency. Besides, we have always been blessed with an able and influential Board of Directors. Very resp'y,

WM. J. QUINLAN, JR.,
Cashier."

The report of this bank, published Oct. 1st, 1885, showed a surplus fund of four millions of dollars. It has been so common in this country for banks to issue money that the impression is quite general that we cannot have banks unless they are permitted to issue money. This impression we see is without foundation.

Nor is banking such a difficult business that only men of extraordinary ability can master it. "Any careful person," says Walter Bagehot, (Lombard Street. p. 256.) "who is experienced in figures, and has real sound sense, may easily make himself a good banker. The modes in which money can be safely lent by a banker are not many, and a clear-headed, quick, industrious person may soon learn all tnat is necessary about them."

The most important Bank in the world is controlled by men not brought up to the business of a banker. "By old usage, the directors of the Bank of England cannot be themselves by trade, bankers. In London, no banker has a chance of being a Bank director, or would even think of attempting to be one." (Lombard Street. p. 212).

CHAPTER XII.

AMOUNT OF MONEY NEEDED.

THE amount of money which our Nation needs to carry on the business of the country cannot be definitely stated. We need more in proportion to the number of inhabitants than old nations, the resources of which are generally developed. We are an active, restless, manufacturing, trading people: and we need more money than we should if we were settled down, contented to quietly earn our living, and nothing more, from the cultivation of the soil. But we raise enormous crops to sell; and we make and sell and buy vast quantities of manufactured articles, and it takes a great deal of money to carry on all this business easily.

1. We should have money enough in the country to do all the work for which money is needed. The attributes of money should not be given to anything but money.

A piece of money carries with it the value

stamped upon it, wherever it goes in the nation that coined it. A dollar *is a dollar*, whether obtained by honest labor, or by gambling, or by robbery.

But this should not be the case with any other paper than paper money. It is not with a deed. A deed carries with it no better title to the property which it assumes to convey than the maker of it possessed. If there is a taint in the title, the deed carries the taint with it. This should be the case with every kind of paper that is used to transfer values, except actual money. There is great need of a radical change in our laws in this respect.

If a promissory note is obtained by fraud, it is worthless in the hands of the man who obained it. He cannot collect it by law. But he sells it to a money shark for half its face, and the new owner readily obtains judgment against the victimized maker, for all that the note calls for, with interest and costs. This opens the way to endless rascality. It encourges villainy in every form that depraved ingenuity can devise.

Similar items to the following, which we clip from to-day's paper, are not uncommon:

"The 'preacher' is the latest swindling dodge being worked in Central Iowa. He ca'ls on his way distributing Bibles, and often presents the family with a handsome book. He then asks for dinner or other meal, and then takes a receipt for twenty-five cents paid for the meal. A few months later the neighboring bank calls for the payment of a note for a large amount."

There are many whose sole business is to obtain money by similar methods. A gentleman in appearance calls upon a farmer and explains to him a valuable farm implement. He appoints him local agent and gets him to sign an apparently harmless contract. Before ninety days are up a money shaver in the adjoining village gives him notice that he holds his promissory note for several hundred dollars! He has given no note, and seeks an explanation. The signature is genuine: he cannot deny it. He finds that when he signed the contract he unwittingly signed a note, artfully concealed. But he is compelled to pay it to the *"innocent"* holder. At one time this fraud was carried on extensively, and hundreds were made victims.

Depraved ingenuity is tasked to the utmost to obtain fraudulent paper for "innocent holders" to collect.

Sometimes whole communities are swindled. A few months ago, fraudulent county bonds were issued in Indiana by rascally officials. They sold these bonds for money, traded them for horses or buggies or any thing they could get in exchange. One of them said in his safe retreat in Canada, that he had issued of these fraudulent bonds enough to fill his room!

In many towns in the State of New York, prominent citizens were hired to go around and get the consent of the tax-payers to bond the town for a proposed railroad. No public meeting was called, no opportunity for discussion was presented. They obtained a majority of the names. The town was bonded for many thousands of dollars. The bonds were sold. But the railroad was never built. There was probably no intention to build it. The Company which obtained the bonds could never collect them, but in the hands of "innocent holders" they must be paid.

It is fully time that the laws in such cases

and all judicial decisions concerning them, were reversed. All commercial paper should be divested of the attributes of money. If a man buys a horse he buys it at his own risk. Though he be an "innocent" purchaser, the sheriff takes it, if the horse was stolen. The buyer of property gets no better title to it than the man had of whom he bought. It should be so in the sale of a promissory note, or of any other evidence of indebtedness. No promissory note, bond, check, draft, or other evidence of indebtedness should acquire any degree of validity by simply passing into the hands of a third party. Any defence of the maker, or indorser, should possess the same virtue against whoever may hold it that it would possess against the party to whom it was given.

It is objected that this would hurt credit. It would hurt the credit of scheming swindlers. But this is precisely what ought to be done. It would close up one of the oldest and most faithfully worked mines of fraud. It would render impossible countless villainies that are practiced upon the unsuspecting, and often even upon experienced men of business, and upon whole communities. It would put a stop to many a scheme to plunder towns and cities under cover of law.

But it would render credit stronger by rendering it safer. It would put a premium upon honesty. Every man who buys any form of credit, would be careful with whom he deals. He would depend upon the responsibility of the party of whom he buys. The same rule should hold in regard to the purchase of what is called "commercial paper" that does in the purchase of other commodities. The maxim of the Civil Law, *Caveat emptor—Let the purchaser beware,* should apply in this, as in other cases. There is a stronger reason for it because of the greater opportunity for fraud. The property of money of carrying a title to it on its face should not be given to any thing else.

Properly speaking, "nothing can perform the functions of money which is not money." (Walker on Money. p. 405.)

The country, then, should be so well supplied with money that there would be no need of substitutes. If any are provided, their circulation should be discouraged by law.

2. The volume of money in circulation should preserve from year to year as nearly as possible the same relative proportion to the number and wants of the people. There should be no violent, arbitrary fluctuations.

Any great inflation of the currency raises the price of property, and in the same proportion, lessens the value of debts. It is an injustice to the class of creditors, and encourages wild speculations.

To contract the currency increases the value of debts, lowers the price of property, and robs debtors by obliging them to sell a greater amount of property to pay their debts. An immense wrong has been done to the American people by contracting the volume of their currency. In this way the value of the national debt was doubled.

Ninety-five members of the last House of Representatives of the United States, say in a letter to the President of the United States, Feb. 11, 1885, "It can be shown that it will take more labor or more of the produce of labor to pay what remains of our national debt now than it would have taken to pay it all at the close of the war. Eighteen million bales of cotton were the equivalent in value of the entire interest bearing debt in 1865, but it will take thirty-five million bales at the price of cotton now to pay the remainder of the debt. Twenty-five million tons of bar iron would have paid the whole debt in 1865. It will now take thirty five million tons to pay what remains after all that has been paid." (North American Review, Nov. 1885, p. 493.)

But individual debtors suffer most from the enhancement of the value of debts they owe. Many industrious men have lost the frugal savings of years, because it took much more of the products of their labor to pay the mortgage on the place they bought, than it did to represent it when the debt was made. Many a home half paid for when bought would not sell a few years after, for enough to pay the balance. If a law were to be enacted saying that a debt made for one hundred dollars, on which interest had been regularly paid, could not be discharged with a less sum than two hundred dollars, it would be seen to be no better than robbery. But this is precisely what is done when the currency of the country is so contracted as to require double the labor to pay a debt that it did when the debt was made. It is legalized robbery.

Jefferson says, "This state is in a condition of unparalleled distress. The sudden reduction of the circulating medium from a plethory to all but annihilation is producing an entire revolution of fortune. In other places, I have known lands sold by the sheriff for one year's rent." (Works v. 7. 151.)

Many cannot understand why there is so much money to be lent when the currency is being contracted. They say that money is plenty because any amount of it can be had on good security. The reason is that nobody who has money is willing to put it into business. One will not buy property only as obliged to, when he knows that the property will depreciate on his hands. The manufacturer properly avoids getting a stock of goods on hand which he must sell for less than it cost to make them. The consequence is that every one who has money, is anxious to loan it on good security. Hence there is this seeming contradiction, when money is scarce in the country generally there is plenty of it on the market in the money centers.

There should be, therefore, not only a plentiful, but also a steady supply of money in the country. It should not be subject to arbitrary variation brought about by the greed of men. When, on some emergency, more than an ordinary amount of money is required, a safe provision should be made to meet the demand.

"There will be," says Alexander Del Mar, (N. A. Review, Nov., 1885), "no settlement of the laws relating to money until the Government assumes entire control of it; and this is what should be done without further delay. The interests of society demand a precise, a stable, an equitable measure of value, and the Government alone can furnish one. The preservation of our national unity invites the exertion of a force which, like that of a uniform money, is all pervading in its influence and constant in its operation. And when we come to the law of the matter, we have only to recall the words of the great Expounder of the Constitution, 'Whenever paper is to perform the functions of coin, its regulation naturally belongs to the hands which hold the power over the coinage.'"

It is impossible to determine, with precision, just how much money a nation should have in circulation. It should have enough to meet all its wants.

"Mr. Mulhall gives the total amount of all kinds of money, gold, silver, and paper, per inhabitant, as, in Britain, five pounds, six shillings; in France, ten pounds, ten shilshillings; in the United States, five pounds fifteen shillings. Holland, a mercantile nation, stands eight pounds five shillings. The nations having little business and no great amount of wealth have small amounts of circulating medium. Russia having only one pound, fifteen shillings, a great part of which is irredeemable paper." (N. A. Review, Nov., 1885.)

According to this estimate, France has almost double the amount of money in circulation, per inhabitant, that the United States has. But that France has none too much is evident from the general prosperity her people enjoy. Notwithstanding the great reverses this nation met with lately in her war with Germany, and the heavy taxes her people have, in consequence, to pay, yet they do not emigrate in such vast numbers as the people do from Germany and Great Britain. In none of our cities are found Frenchmen, who have recently left their native land, in sufficient numbers to become the ruling power in the city. The difference in the amount of the circulating medium in these European countries is one great cause of the great difference in the relative contentment of their people.

This young and growing country needs relatively more money for general circulation than France does. But France evidently has none too much. Then we have far too little. A greater supply is needed to develop the natural resources of the country, and to put and keep our manufacturing industries in motion. To use what we have to advantage we need more. It would be hard for a man to make his living on the best farm with nothing but his hands. But

AMOUNT OF MONEY NEEDED.

give him team and tools and seed, and he will have plenty of produce to spare. A vast amount of money is invested in costly machinery in manufactories. More money is needed to keep them in operation and to prevent what is invested from becoming a dead loss.

Our population is rapidly increasing, and the Government should make provision to furnish the nation with an increase of money for its use in proportion to its increase in population. The banks should not have the power to do this; and they could not be depended on to do it if they had. As Andrew Jackson well said, "The banks cannot be relied upon to keep the currency uniform in amount." THE PEOPLE should require Congress to faithfully perform the duty imposed upon it by the Constitution, and furnish them with a proper amount of good, reliable money.

CHAPTER XIII.

"ELASTIC CURRENCY."

IN any given locality more money is needed at some seasons than at others to transact its business with facility. In some of our counties many thousands of dollars are paid out in the fall of the year for apples, in the winter for wheat; in others in the spring for cattle, and wool, and cotton. Hence some maintain that the quantity of money in the country should be variable—that it should be easy to put more money in circulation or to retire a surplus as demanded by the fluctuations of trade. Hence it has been proposed that Government bonds bearing a low rate of interest, and paper money issued by the Government, be interchangeable with each other. Then, if there is more money than is needed, it could be changed into bonds; if there is less than is needed, the bonds could be changed for money.

To this plausible plan there are fatal objections.

First, the prosperity of the country would be at the mercy of capitalists. They could, by combination, expand or contract the volume of money in circulation at their will. The prices of commodities and the value of debts would be in their hands. It would depend upon their edict whether the farmer would have to pay for a machine which he bought on credit a hundred bushels of wheat, or two hundred bushels of wheat. This is a power too dangerous to be placed in the hands of any class of men. This country has had a bitter experience of the readiness of a favored class to unsettle values whenever they can do it to their own advantage. This of itself is a sufficient objection to the proposed arrangement.

Second, the National Government should not be in debt. It should "owe no man any thing." The paper money which it issues should be as good as gold and silver, but it should be money, and not a promise to pay; therefore it would not be a debt.

The fashion of going into debt should not

be set by the supreme authority of the land. States and cities and towns are burdened with debts. The custom of going into debt for improvements leads to extravagance and villainy. Many a public work built on credit cost double of what it would if it had been paid for as it was carried on. Those who vote expenditures of money should pay their proportion of the expenditure. "Improvements" not needed are often projected because those who project them manage to have others pay for them. States and cities and towns are burdened with debts that never should have been contracted.

It would greatly improve the government of our cities and towns if they were obliged to pay their expenses as they go along, and if their local elections could be held the next week after the payment of taxes.

But is it really necessary that money should be "elastic." to any considerable extent?

A farmer needs more teams when getting in his crops than at other seasons of the year. But he does not ordinarily buy more horses. He works to the best advantage all that he has. Some of his teams do double the work that they do at other seasons. So, when money is specially needed, it should be made to do more service by being more active.

Bishop Berkeley pertinently inquires, "Whether six-pence twice paid be not as good as a shilling once paid?"

The amount of paper money should be kept within fixed limits. In an exigency, enough unused metal suitable for coin can be brought forth to meet the demand.

It is said that Napoleon, finding in a church some statues made of silver, inquired what they were. The priests replied that they were statues of the twelve apostles. "Then," said the Emperor, "like their Master, they should be going about doing good." He ordered them to be melted up and coined into money.

Prof. Frances A. Walker writes so sensibly on this point that we quote him at some length. He says, (Money p. 416.) "Those who demand that money shall be 'elastic,' mean by this, that there shall be more of it at one time than at another. Is this elasticity? A rubber band is elastic, but there is no more of it at one time than at another. It will cover more ground at one time than at another, but it only does so by becoming thinner. There will be more of it, in any one place, at one time than at another, but for this reason, there is less of it in some other place. There is no more rubber when the band is stretched than there was before. Now, elasticity in this, the true sense, belongs eminently to metallic money. No class of commodities, known to men, yield more quickly under pressure, or re-act more promptly. If an exceptional demand arises anywhere, gold or silver responds with an alacrity which would be unattainable by any article not possessing great value for its bulk, and not, at the same time that article in which the values of all commodities are expressed for purposes of exchange. But while, in obedience to economical impulses, however slight, there may be more of such money in any one place at one time than another, the total amount is not on that account, increased. There is less at the same time in some other places, or in all other places.

This fact is essential to create that tension which shall make it certain that, when the exceptional demand in the first indicated place shall cease, the volume of money will be promptly and accurately redistributed according to the prevailing conditions of international commerce."

Money, like labor, will make its own way to any place where there is a special demand for it. It is not necessary to create more money to meet a temporary demand. For, as Prof. Walker says, (Money p.448.) "First. The periodical occasions for a larger use of money, on the part of different trades and different localities, go far to offset each other. The busy time of the manufacturer is not necessarily the busy time of the agriculturist; lumber and cotton are not moved to market in the same season In the same way trade reaches its height in different sections and countries at different periods of the year, so that money may be doing its work this month in France, return next month to England to meet the demands of Lancashire, and go two weeks later to Glasgow, in the usual November drain northward, to satisfy the wants of the iron trade of Scotland.

"Secondly. It does not follow from the fact that more exchanges are to be effected by the use of money that more actual pounds or dollars are requisite. Money is a quantity of two dimensions,—the number of pieces of gold, or silver, or paper, and their rate of movement. A scarcity of money will first make itself felt in an increased activity of what is on hand. Each piece will accomplish more payments in the same time. A rising rate of interest makes the use of money worth more, and hence it will not be allowed to remain so long idle in the pocket or the drawer. If the merchant or the manufacturer has to pay eight per cent. in place of six for discounts, he will calculate his outgoings and incomings more closely, in order to reduce the average amount lying in his till. He will deposit more promptly to secure the higher interest; he will take more pains in collecting sums due from his customers, with whom the money might otherwise have tarried a day or a week longer.

"Thirdly. While there is a tendency, in a normal condition of production and trade, to a greater demand for money at one period than at another, a certain stringency at such times is desirable as exerting a wholesome repression upon speculative movements. The present industrial and commercial organization of the world powerfully tends to gather production into great waves with corresponding intervals of depression—overproduction succeeded surely by stagnation. A certain waste of energy, which always results from fitful exertions, must be accepted as among the economical conditions of this age. But it is utterly undesirable that the tendency should be quickened and strengthened by the facility of issues of local origin and circulation."

The main thing necessary for this country is to have a sufficient volume of money, and there will be no difficulty in meeting a special demand in any particular place.

CHAPTER XIV.
DISTRIBUTION OF MONEY.

MONEY, as the representative of value, will go where there is something of value to be exchanged for it. It is given for labor, and for the products of labor and skill. The great centers of wealth are great money centers.

If a man has money, but engages in no remunerative labor or business, those who labor for him will, in time, honestly obtain his money. Spain, possessed of the mines of Mexico and Peru, the richest in the world, became the poorest among the great nations of Europe; "owing to the accumulation of estates in the hands of communities and noble families, and the predominant influence of the Catholic priesthood, which for centuries had rendered that fine kingdom little else than a cluster of convents surrounded by a hardy peasantry." (Alison's Hist. of Europe, vol. 1, p. 168.)

No matter how widely money may be scattered, it returns to those who own the property, as naturally as running water returns to the ocean. It is in the order of nature that to "him that hath shall be given, and he shall have more abundance."

That money may be generally distributed among the people it is necessary that property, for which money is given, should be distributed.

It is impossible that there should be an equality of property among a people free to act and possessing an equality of rights. If an equal division of the property of the country were made among the people, there would be great difference in the amounts which different persons would possess in a year afterward. In the old Jewish republic, the greatest possible precautions were taken that each family should possess a competence. The land was divided among them. Every one had a farm, a homestead, in the country. If one was compelled to sell his inheritance, he could alienate it from his family for only fifty years at the longest. At the year of jubilee debts were cancelled and inheritances restored. Yet in their palmiest days they had their poor among them. But they had none, while the republic lasted, enormously rich, and probably none who suffered from poverty. All, while obedient to God, were in comfortable circumstances.

It is better for the families and better for the country in every respect, that the farms be owned by the persons working them, than that one man own a county, and all the other men in it work for him. The few immense farms in the Northwest are a curse to the community in which they are situated. No pleasant homes are made. Schools and churches are not founded and sustained. The farms are worked by tramps and vagrants who leave the country as soon as the season is over, and they get their pay.

The sole interest the owners feel in their farms is to make all the money off from them that they possibly can. They put on as little as possible and take off all that is possible.

Good order and general prosperity prevail in our cities in proportion as the business is divided up among the inhabitants. The greater the proportion of men who work for others, the greater danger there is of riotous disturbances. It is as advantageous to the city, as it is to the country, to have the property and the business divided up among a large number of owners.

In this country there are two strong reasons why every provision consistent with the rights of all should be made for the general distribution of money among the people.

First, *our laws* establish *manhood suffrage*. In deciding who shall rule over us, one is given as much influence as another. The millionaire casts no mightier a ballot than the pauper. In feudal times, when one was made a lord he was given an ample domain to maintain his dignity. So, now, those who determine what protection shall be given to property, should have some property to protect. When it gets to the point that one class of men vote taxes which another class of men are compelled to pay, the Government will be little better than a legalized conspiracy against private as well as public property.

Second, the State provides the means of education for all the people. It is expected that all born on American soil shall be enlightened. Any one, no matter what may be his condition, may obtain, if he has the determination and the ability, a respectable education. It is often the case that the young man who works out, is better educated than the man who employs him. His tastes and instincts are higher. A people thus educated, NEED MONEY to purchase the comforts and conveniences of life which have become a necessity to them. They cannot be happy and contented in a condition of poverty that might be endurable by a people who never possessed their advantages. The Government, in giving the masses education, obligates itself to afford them all reasonable facilities for acquiring the competence which it has fitted them to enjoy, and to keep them from that biting poverty which it has unfitted them to endure.

He who teaches the savage to gain his living with the plow and hoe, instead of with the bow and arrow, should render it possible for him to obtain the plow and hoe. If the nation educates the people so that good clothes and comfortable houses are a necessity, then it should render it possible for them to obtain good clothes and comfortable houses.

The very least that our Government can do, with safety, is to give to all its citizens, as far as possible, an equal facility for making money. There should be no favorites; there should be none proscribed.

France was able to put down her communistic war, because the great mass of her people are property holders. It pays the German war indemnity, and thrives under it, better than Germany does in receiving it, because all her people have money. It has, as we have seen, more money in proportion to its population than any other nation in the world.

There is, in France, compared with other nations, a remarkably equal distribution of property among her people. This is owing largely to the nature of her laws.

The tendency of our laws is in the opposite direction. Under their influence, the rich are made richer, and the poor poorer. There have probably been more vast fortunes accumulated in the United States during the last quarter of a century than in any other nation of the world. This has been done under the operation of laws fostering it. The favorable conditions created by law have contributed largely to this result. All such laws should be changed.

These vast accumulations of fortune in the hands of a few are detrimental and dangerous to the people at large. They are not obtained by honest industry or beneficent skill. The farmer who raises a thousand bushels of wheat, or the manufacturer who makes a thousand yards of cloth, adds so much to the actual wealth of the country. But he who, in carrying their wheat to the market takes from each of ten thousand farmers ten bushels of wheat more than his services are actually worth, simply enriches himself at their expense. Thousands are deprived of needed comforts that he may revel in luxury. Discontent and anarchy are created. Now and then, riots break out as an indirect result of the unequal distribution of gains among those by whose labor they were made. The way is gradually being paved to a terrible, communistic war. All laws which specially favor the gaining and the holding of great fortunes should be changed. Among such laws are those relating to

1. *The gift of franchises.* A company of men are given by statute the right to build a railroad through other men's lands. This right is one created by law. It is not one of the *jura natura*—*natural* rights of mankind. It is an interference with the rights of many for the benefit of a few, under the plea that it is for the public good. It is conferred by the state by positive enactments, and should be regulated by the state. A railroad or a ferry is not private property in the sense that a farm or a house is private property. *All franchises given by the state should be distributed by the state.* The men who make themselves rich from one franchise should not be allowed, out of its profits, to buy up others that come in competition

with it. For example, there should be a constitutional enactment which would prevent the owners of the New York Central Railroad from owning any interest in the Erie or the West Shore. Let the special privileges which the state gives be divided among many. Because one man has been given an advantage over the rest of the community that is no reason why he should be given another.

When a sufficient amount has been realized from a franchise to pay for all that has been expended in rendering it productive, and a reasonable profit in addition, it should then revert to the state. Corporations created by the state, and endowed with special privileges by it, should not be allowed to go on, and out of the community at large, pile up wealth indefinitely for the individual benefit of those who may be in control. Such privileges are dangerous. They will make trouble. Already in some of the states it is said that the railroad corporations control the successive Legislatures, whether they be Republican or Democratic, in all matters affecting their interests, as absolutely as they do their engineers and conductors. The change of the party in power does not change the policy of the state towards these wealthy corporations. Enactments are made giving them advantages which would be considered as little better than grand or petit larceny in other kinds of business. It is time that a stop was put to the making of laws in the interests of rich corporations against the common rights of the people. The hard-working farmers in some of the most productive sections of our country are kept poor by the exactions of the railroads on which they depend to get their produce to the market.

2. *Joint Stock Companies.* The laws creating and governing these popular companies appear to be made wholly in the interest of the rich and the unscrupulous.

One who owns or controls a majority of the stock has as absolute control as if he owned the whole. He decides who shall be the officers and what shall be their salaries. He makes sales or mortgages at his will.

A railroad is projected. People living along the line are urged to take stock.

Many do so. The road, when completed, is successful. But it is mortgaged, ostensibly to raise money to pay floating debts. In due time it is sold under the mortgage, and the small stockholders lose every dollar they put in. It is said that the only ones who did not come out millionaires from building one of our great railroads were those who had paid up their subscriptions for stock.

The inhabitants of a thriving town are persuaded that it would add greatly to the business of the place and to the value of the property in it, to have a smelting furnace, or a sewing machine factory, or agricultural works. All who can be, are influenced to take stock in the new enterprise. It succeeds even better than was expected. But those who have a controlling interest are not satisfied with their large salaries and large profits. They desire to absorb the whole. They adopt a system of annoyance which the laws render not only possible but easy, and compel the small stockholders to sell out on such terms as those having a controlling interest may dictate. In this way aged men and women who had saved enough to make them comfortable and were anxious to make a profitable investment have lost all their money. The laws governing joint-stock companies should be so amended as to protect the rights of small stockholders.

3. *Stock Gambling.* Many large fortunes are made by manipulating stocks. But where one makes, many others lose. Where one becomes a millionaire, thousands are reduced to poverty. It is a great loss to to a country, when the sharpest, most far-seeing, capable men, instead of engaging in some useful pursuit, devote all their energies to gambling.

A man buys a million bushels of wheat to be delivered in three months. Neither of the parties to the transaction owns a bushel of wheat and does not expect to. When the time for delivering the wheat comes, if the market price is higher than it was when the purchase was made, the seller pays the difference; if it is lower the purchaser pays the difference. The whole transaction is simply a bet that wheat will be worth so much at a given time. Stocks are bought in the same way. All such trading in margins should be strictly prohibited by law.

4. *Monopolies.* Brain work is entitled to its just compensation as really as manual labor. He who invents any thing useful should be recompensed for his invention. Hence, our laws on patents give to the patentee of any article a monoply for its manufacture and sale for a limited number of years. He can fix his own price and shut out all competition. The profits on some patented articles are simply enormous. He who started poor becomes in a few years a millionaire.

The same law that creates a monopoly should fix a reasonable limit to the amount that may be realized from it. When that amount is reached, the monopoly should terminate, and the public reap the benefit of the invention. No unnatural facilities should be afforded by the law to take money from the many for the benefit of the few. In all ages monopolies have been a source of dissatisfaction and contention. Every thing tending to create or maintain a monopoly should be looked upon with a jealous eye.

"Monopolies," says Adam Smith, "derange more or less the natural distribution of the stock of the society." (Wealth of Nations, p. 493.)

Many of the bad results of monopolies are produced by the combinations which at present are so popular. Nearly all the great productive industries of the country, except the agricultural, are combined. There is a systematic interference with the law that prices should be regulated by supply and demand. Whenever this interference prevails, disastrous results are sure to follow. The prices of manufactured articles are generally regulated by the arbitary agreements of the manufacturers. The price of the article in question is put a little lower than it could be sold in our market if bought in Europe, and the amount which must be paid for duties and transportation added. But little reference is had to its cost here.

The workmen, perceiving that they do not have their share of the products of their labor, follow the example of their employers, and form combinations to secure larger prices for less labor. Fierce antagonisms are provoked, and business derangements and family sufferings follow.

The actual cost of manufacturing goods in this country, under our present system, is such that we cannot, to any great extent, compete with other nations where we meet upon an equal footing. But such are our natural advantages that we ought to be able to undersell all other manufacturing and commercial nations. We have water power sufficient to run all the machinery of the world. Our mines of iron and coal are apparently inexhaustible, and are easily reached. Cotton, and wool, and lumber, and other raw materials are produced in abundance. We can furnish supplies of food to feed all who come. Our great rivers, and lakes, and numerous railroads furnish every facility for cheap transportation. Yet with all these advantages, our trade with our next door neighbors in Mexico and Central America and South America is small. They depend mainly upon Europe for their manufactured goods. We are pretty nearly shut out of the market of the world. This is brought about by purely

DISTRIBUTION OF MONEY.

artificial means which have the effect of monopolies in raising prices above the natural standard. As a result, our manufacturers are obliged to depend almost wholly upon the home market. But the same cause limits the ability of the purchasers in the home market, to buy. Their purchases would be much larger if they had the means with which to pay.

Suppose a dozen families live on a remote island, shut off from all communication with the rest of the world. One half of them are mechanics, and one half farmers. The mechanics combine, and say that their labor is skilled labor. They will therefore require two days work of the farmer for one of their own. If this agreement is carried out, the mechanics must, of necessity, lie still half the time. There is no help for it. This is essentially the state of things in this country. About one half the people are farmers. Every one of them could use a thousand dollars worth of goods a year if he had the means with which to buy them; but as he has not, he can get along with a much smaller amount.

Those who make his tools, and furniture,

and cloth have procured the enactment of laws that compel him to buy his supplies of them. Then, by combining together, they compel him to give the product of two or more days of his labor for the product of one day's labor of their own. Yet, as farms and factories are now carried on, the farm labor is of the two, skilled labor. It takes a longer time to learn to run a farm successfully than it does to learn to run a machine in a manufactory.

On an average, the farmer gives more than two days of his labor to pay for one day's labor of the man who made the goods he buys. Hence this man must go unemployed more than half the time. It is unavoidable. Every autumn, it is confidently asserted that there is to be a revival of business because there is an abundant harvest. But business does not revive. Thousands go unemployed, a large portion of the time. There will be a comparative stagnation of business as long as these two conditions exist. First, while the currency is being contracted from year to year. Second, while the equilibrium of prices is destroyed by artificial combinations which amount to a monopoly. We may have every other element of prosperity but while these two causes continue in operation the wheels of business will drag heavily.

It is sought to justify these substantial monopolies on the ground that they are in the interest of our workmen, and are intended to protect them from competition with the pauper labor of Europe. But monopolies are not intended for the protection of laborers. As Adam Smith justly says, "It is the industry which is carried on for the benefit of the rich and the powerful that is principally encouraged by our mercantile system. That which is carried on for the poor and the indigent, is too often either neglected or oppressed." (Wealth of Nations p. 504.) The workingmen in the woolen manufactories of England receive much better wages now than they did when the importation of woolen cloths from any foreign country was absolutely prohibited, and when, by the 8th Eliz., chap. 3, "The exporter of sheep, lambs, or rams, was for the first offence to forfeit all his goods forever, to suffer a year's imprisonment, and then to have his left hand cut off in a market town upon a market day, to be there nailed up; and for the second offence to be adjudged a felon, and to suffer death accordingly." (Ibid 507.) The best encouragement that can be given to manufacturers is to furnish them with a plenty of prompt paying consumers. "Consumption is the sole end and purpose of all production; and the interest of the producer ought to be attended to, only so far as it may be necessary for promoting that of the consumer. The maxim is so perfectly self-evident that it would be absurd to attempt to prove it. But in the mercantile system, the interest of the consumer is almost constantly sacrificed to that of the producer; and it seems to consider production, and not consumption, as the ultimate end and object of all industry and commerce." (Ibid p. 517.) Monopolies, whatever may be their form, operate against the welfare of the community at large.

5. *Laws of Inheritance.* In nations which have a hereditary nobility it is consistent that the heir to the title should be the heir to the bulk of the property. In England

the eldest son is the heir. The law that secures this is called "The law of Primogeniture." It originated under the feudal system, in the dark ages. Landed property was given to men renowned in arms, and was held on condition of their rendering military services to their chief. When the father died, the eldest son was generally best fitted to take his place on the field of battle. "The eldest son," says the Hon. G. C. Brodrick, in "Law of Primogeniture," "therefore, was invested with his exceptional privileges under the feudal system, not because he was supposed to have any exceptional rights, but rather because he was supposed to be the most eligible for the performance of exceptional duties." In England this developed into the Law of Primogeniture. By this law and that of "Entail," large estates are kept in the same families, especially in those of the nobility, from generation to generation. But such laws are not popular with the common people. The writer last referred to says, "Rich capitalists who do not invest in land, or aspire to found a county family, seldom make an 'eldest son,' (that is chief heir) and of those who do indulge this ambition, some prefer to buy a moderate estate for each of their sons. Still more habitually is equal division recognized as the dictate of natural equity by the great body of merchants, tradespeople, and professional men, as well as by the laboring classes throughout Great Britain and Ireland; in short, by the middle and lower orders of society, 'divorced from the soil' in this country, and by the landless members of the upper orders." (Land Tenure p. 374.)

The founders of our government were aware of the incompatibility of large hereditary fortunes with free institutions. They endeavored to guard against them by abolishing the Law of Primogeniture and the law of Entail. But experience proves that this is not sufficient. We need, in addition, something like the French law of succession. This law "limits the parental power of testamentary disposition over property to a part equal to one child's share, and divides the remainder among the children equally." (Land tenure. p. 290.) If there are five children, the property is divided into six parts.

In any event each of the five children gets one of these parts. The parent can dispose of but one of these parts by will. This right, it is said, is seldom exercised. In France, the law also favors the transfer of land by purchase.

As a consequence of the law dividing estates upon the death of the owner, and the law enabling one to purchase land at but little cost for transferring the title, the common people have generally become land owners. It is said that there are in England two hundred and fifty thousand owners of real estate;—in France, from four to five millions. The people are prosperous and contented to a degree not found in any other nation of Europe. "Those who have studied the condition of the French cultivators not merely in books, but in their own country, and who have witnessed the improvements which have taken place in it and in their cultivation year after year, will probably regard the number with a feeling of satisfaction. One thing, at least, is established by it, that property in land is, in France, a national possession; that the territory of the nation belongs to the nation, and that no national revolution can take place for the destruction of private property." (LandTenure, p. 289.)

Our laws should make provision for the breaking up of great estates upon the death of the owners. The steady aim of our Government should be to afford to all, every just and proper facility for acquiring a moderate competence. To do this, the whole bent of our laws must be unfavorable to the acquisition of a vast amount of property by any one person, and to the handing of it down unbroken from generation to generation.

CHAPTER XV.//
HOW TO MAKE MONEY.

IT is a gross caricature of Christianity to represent that it teaches that happiness in the future world is to be secured by neglecting the duties which we owe to our fellow men in the present world. It teaches quite the contrary. It insists upon the faithful performance of all the duties we owe to others in every relation of life. Nor is the prohibition to lay up for ourselves treasures on earth any exception. We must provide for our own wants, so as not to be chargeable to any; but we must not heap up riches that can do us no good. "But if any provide not for his own, and specially for those of his own house, he hath denied the faith and is worse than an infidel."—1 Tim. 5: 8.

It is right, then for any man to secure a moderate competence. How may it be done honestly and in the fear of God?

Perhaps a better business manual cannot be found than the book of Proverbs. It contains practical directions which, if followed out, can hardly fail of securing success in business.

We offer a few suggestions to those who would make money in a way consistent with their happiness in this world and in the world to come.

1. *Do not aim at getting rich.* Money is valuable, only as a means to secure some worthy end. It is useful, only because of what it can secure. Money is neither food nor clothing. Midas, at whose touch every thing turned to gold, was obliged, in order to keep from starving, to beg to have the coveted gift recalled. The favor of God, an upright character, good health, confiding friends, go farther than riches towards securing happiness. These, money cannot buy. Not the slightest sacrifice of any of these should ever be made for the sake of making money. The aim should be to do our duty to God, to our fellow men, and to ourselves. If this is faithfully done, a competence will ordinarily follow in the order of events. But

if one bends his energies to money-making, he is in great danger of sacrificing something more valuable than money in order to obtain it. "But they that will be rich fall into temptation and a snare, and into many foolish, and hurtful lusts, which drown men in destruction and perdition." 1 Tim. 6: 9.

2. *Be diligent in business.* Man was made for work. His constitution fits him for it. His health requires it. We have no right to place ourselves, or others, not even our children, in a condition in which there is no need of working. Those who make the pursuit of pleasure the business of life, are, as a class, both useless and unhappy. "Six days shalt tou labor and do all thy work," is as binding as the other part of the command, "Remember the Sabbath day to keep it holy."

"When I was a boy," said a successful merchant, "I was set, with another boy, to watch my grandfather's sheep on the mountains of Vermont. The other boy was intent on amusing himself. I had to look after the sheep. I complained to my grandfather. He heard me patiently and then said, 'Never mind. You mind the sheep and you will own the sheep.' I thought it over. What can he mean? I own the sheep! It seemed impossible. But I did. He gave me one. I added to it, and while I was yet a young boy I owned a flock. I learned thus early that to own a business one must attend to the business."

Let a young man of good ability work for others. If he is steady and industrious and looks faithfully after the interest of his employers as if the business were his own, he will, in a few years, probably have an interest in the business.

The wages which one receives are a secondary matter. High wages do not of necessity furnish the means to own a home. Right around us are fine, costly farms, owned by men yet in their prime, who began by working out by the month on a farm. They never received high wages. They began perhaps at ten dollars a month, and never received, except for a few days in harvest, over a dollar a day. While they worked out, their wages would not average that. But they were faithful. In a few years they saved enough to enable them to work a farm on shares. They laid by enough to make a good payment down, and then bought a farm, and in a few years finished paying for it.

Many a large business concern is owned by men who began in it poor. *"He becometh poor that dealeth with a slack hand; but the hand of the diligent maketh rich."*—Prov. 10. 4. "Seest thou a man diligent in his business? he shall stand before kings; he shall not stand before mean men."— Prov. 22: 29.

3. *Be careful about going into debt.* Never go into debt for any thing that will not stand as security for the debt, and which will not furnish you with means to pay it. Live within your income, no matter how small that may be. Wear the old hat, and the old coat until you can pay for a new one. If you are working for wages lay by something regularly out of your wages. Ordinarily you can do this, if you will. If you rent a house, buy one as soon as you have saved enough to make a payment, and then pay towards it every month what you would

otherwise pay for rent. In such a case, it is not so much yourself as the property that is incumbered with debt. Avoid all mere speculations. Have nothing to do with stock gambling and dealing in margins. But it is proper, and often wise, to buy real estate if the income from it will pay interest and taxes, as it is altogether probable that it will rise in value.

4. *Never become responsible for the debts of others.* Many, who, by industry and frugality had laid by a competence, have in their old age, been reduced to poverty by indorsing for others. Mr. Forester and his wife came from England thirty years ago. He worked in a mill, bought him a pleasant home of a few acres, and had enough money laid by so that they could live comfortably the rest of their days. He then retired from business. An old friend from the same neighborhood in England owned the next farm to his. They had been intimate for years. This old friend wanted him to sign a note of eight thousand dollars with him for three months. He yielded to his persuasions. The man for whom he signed had secretly

put his property out of his hands, and the indorser had the note to pay. His home was sold on execution, every thing that the law could take was taken; and now, nearly eighty years old he gets such jobs to do as he can, and his aged wife goes out washing to keep from starving.

My friend, Mr. Gilroy, was a prosperous farmer. His farm was near town, had been brought to a high state of cultivation and had become valuable. He had good buildings and was out of debt. His sons were well educated young men, full of ambition and enterprise. They could not wait to get rich in the old, plodding way. They engaged in large business enterprises, and got their father to indorse for them. They drew him in gradually; and then, to save what he had risked, he risked more. In a few years they were all left penniless. The pressure upon him was too great, his health gave way, and he went down in sorrow to an untimely grave.

If you wish to help a friend, by giving him a sum of money, do so, if you can afford to. But do not indorse for any one for an amount that you cannot lose without distressing yourself or others. In becoming security for another, you not only indorse his honesty, but also his business ability, and often you take the risk for him as well as for yourself of having unfavorable seasons, and of having hard times brought on by artificial as well as natural causes. It is a risk that no one ought to assume. "Be not thou one of them that strike hands, or of them that are sureties for debts."—Prov. 22: 26.

5. *Maintain good habits.* The great enemy of the workingmen of this country is not the capitalist but the saloon keeper. It takes but a little time to spend the largest salary or the largest fortune at the bar and at the gambling table.

Ex-Governor and ex-Senator Sprague of Rhode Island spent a fortune of twelve million dollars in twenty years. From being an acknowledged leader in business, society, and politics, he became a poor, degraded, base sensualist. His drunken brutality drove from him his devoted, accomplished wife, daughter of the honored Chief Justice Chase.

But other habits besides the drinking habit keep men in poverty. Theatre going, costly entertainments, cigar smoking and tobacco using keep many poor.

"In early life," says a New York merchant, "I smoked six cigars a day, at six and a half cents each ; they averaged that. I thought to myself one day: 'I'll just put aside all the money I am consuming in cigars, and all I would consume if I went on in this habit, and I will see what it will come to by compound interest.' Last July completed thirty-nine years since, by the grace of God, I was emancipated from the filthy habit, and the savings amounted to the enormous sum of $29,102.03 by compound interest. We lived in the city; but the children, who had learned something of country life from their annual visits to their grandparents, longed for a home among the green fields. I noticed a very pleasant place in the country for sale. The cigar money now came into requisition, and I found that it was large enough to purchase the place, and it is mine. I wish all could see how my children enjoy their home."

. You say you wish to enjoy life as you go along; but that is a poor kind of enjoyment which undermines the health. That tobacco does this has been sadly demonstrated.

Says the London *Lancet*, one of the ablest medical journals in the world. "The influence of tobacco is apparently cumulative. A warning sense of excess in the use of tobacco generally comes too late."

Only a few of the more resolute ones heed the premonitory warning. Says Chauncy M. Depew, President of the New York Central railroad: "I was a confirmed smoker, smoking twenty cigars a day, up to about a dozen years ago, when I gave up the habit. I now do not use tobacco. Twelve or thirteen years ago I found myself suffering from indigestion, with wakeful fits at night, nervousness and inability to submit to much mental strain. I was walking up Broadway. I took the cigar out of my mouth and looked at it. I had smoked about an inch of it. A thought struck me. I had been reading a German savant's book on the unhealthfulness of the use of tobacco. I looked at my cigar and I said, 'you are responsible for this mischief.' I threw it into the gutter and resolved not to smoke again. For six months

I suffered the torments of the damned. I wanted to smoke but I resolutely refused. My appetite meanwhile was growing better, my sleep was growing sounder and I could do more work.

"I found the use of tobacco was affecting my physical system and I stopped it entirely and have not commenced it again and probably never shall."

If you maintain good habits you will naturally keep good company. This has, in many ways, much to do with one's success in life. Said the great merchant already referred to, "When I began business for myself as a merchant, according to the custom of that time, I went to New York to buy a bill of goods on credit. I reached there on Saturday, was invited by —— to stay with him over the Sabbath. I did so, and went with him to church all day. Monday morning I started out to make my purchases. I found goods and prices that suited me, at a large wholesale house. I spoke to the proprietor of opening an account and offered to show him my recommendations, of which I had a good supply. He said he did not want to see them,—he was ready to trust me.

"But," I urged, "I am a stranger in the city."

"Did you not," he asked, "go to church yesterday with Mr. ——, and sit with him in his pew?"

"I did."

"Any man who goes to church with Mr. ——, and sits with him, can have all the goods he wants out of my store on credit."

"I saw then that a man's credit is affected by the company he keeps."

6. *Be willing to commence business on a small scale.* Follow up great rivers and you will find they come from little brooks. Many of the large business enterprises of this country had small beginnings. The late A. T. Stewart, the great merchant prince, taught school until he earned enough to start a small store. He raised up a business that his successors, though trained by himself, could not carry on successfully. The Remington Works, which, at one time, employed a small army of men, originated in a common blacksmith shop. The founder ham-

mered out for himself at the anvil a gun-barrel of such excellence that others wanted him to make one like it for them. So many orders came in that he was obliged to construct machinery to enable him to fill them; and the works gradually grew to mammoth proportions.

Many of our great papers were started by men who posessed a talent for hard work but had very little money. Horace Greely, a journeyman printer, without capital, founded the New York *Tribune*, and left it, when he died, worth one million dollars. Mr. Bennett started the New York *Herald* without capital, and was its sole editor, reporter and business manager, and now it is said it could not be bought for five million dollars. The Philadelphia *Ledger* was started by three workingmen whose capital was their intelligence and industry and they thus founded a newspaper concern worth, it is said, three million dollars.

7. *Be benevolent in the use of money.* It takes but little to supply the wants of one. A man is never fully a man till he begins to care for others.

Systematic benevolence aids one to be systematic in business and thus in itself it contributes to success. "There is that scattereth, and yet increaseth; and there is that withholdeth more than is meet, but it tendeth to poverty."—Prov. 11: 24.

Baron Rothschild had the following maxims framed and hung up in his banking house:

"Attend carefully to the details of your business.

Be prompt in all things.

Consider well, then decide positively.

Dare to do right. Fear to do wrong.

Endure trials patiently.

Fight life's battles bravely, manfully.

Go not into the society of the vicious.

Hold integrity sacred.

Injure not another's reputation or business.

Join hands only with the virtuous.

Keep your mind from evil thoughts.

Lie not for any consideration.

Make few acquaintances.

Never try to appear what you are not.

Observe good manners.

Pay your debts promptly.
Question not the veracity of a friend.
Respect the counsel of your parents.
Sacrifice money rather than principle.
Touch not, taste not, handle not intoxicating drinks.
Use your leisure time for improvement.
Venture not upon the threshold of wrong.
Watch carefully over your passions.
Extend to every one a kindly salutation.
Yield not to discouragements.
Zealously labor for the right. Success is yours."

To these maxims add John Wesley's three rules:

1. Gain all you can.
2. Save all you can.
3. Give all you can.

CHAPTER XVI.

CONCLUSION.

THE money question is one that every intelligent American citizen who aims to cast a conscientious ballot should endeavor to understand. It is in his power to comprehend it and he should give it a careful, candid investigation.

2. All money, no matter of what material it is composed, is constituted money by the supreme authority of the land. Neither silver nor gold, until it is duly coined, is money, any more than farms, or cattle, or diamonds are money. Any one may buy them that chooses, but no one is obliged to take them in payment of debt.

3. Both gold and silver should be used for making our metallic money. To stop the coinage of silver would act oppressively upon every class in the community except creditors. It would double the value of all debts, National, State, municipal, and private, and

would cause a general derangement and prostration of business. In its effects it would be legalized robbery. No limit should be put upon the coinage of silver any more than upon that of gold. But no nation which has depreciated the value of silver in the general market by demonetizing it should be allowed to take advantage of our continuing to coin silver and so get a higher price for the silver it has to sell than it will bring in the market of the world. This they might do under a system of "free coinage." Between the years 1873 and 1879 Germany sold 3220 tons of silver. But as our government buys the silver which it coins, at the market price of bullion, England and Germany can get no more for their silver here than they can elsewhere. They cannot, as far as we are concerned, take advantage of their wrong. As they can get no more for their silver here than they can elsewhere, we are in no danger of any great influx of silver from those countries.

4. All paper money should be issued by the National government. The amount which it may issue should be restricted and

kept within such limits that it will always be as good as gold or silver. The Government should issue paper certificates for all the gold and silver, either in coin or bullion, that may be deposited with it.

5. There should be an ample supply of money to meet all the wants of the people. Nothing but money should be allowed to possess the attribute of money. An end should be put to the countless villainies that are practiced by reason of giving to evidences of indebtedness a degree of validity in the hands of third parties which they would not possess if held by those to whom they were given.

6. Our laws should make it difficult for one man to amass a vast fortune and keep it in his family from generation to generation. The property of the country should be held by the people at large.

7. The people should see to it that their representatives in Congress pass laws in their interest, and not in favor of the moneyed class and rich corporations to the injury of community generally. "Eternal vigilance is the price of liberty."

www.ingramcontent.com/pod-product-compliance
Lightning Source LLC
Chambersburg PA
CBHW030302170426
43202CB00009B/842